Living with
dormice

Living with dormice

The Common Dormouse: Real Rodent or Phantom of the Ancient Wood?

Sue Eden

PAPADAKIS

I dedicate this book to my husband, Roy, for all his help and support over so many years

First published in Great Britain in 2009 by
Papadakis Publisher

PAPADAKIS

An imprint of New Architecture Group Limited

HEAD OFFICE: Kimber Studio, Winterbourne, Berkshire, RG20 8AN
DESIGN STUDIO & RETAIL: 11 Shepherd Market, Mayfair, London, W1J 7PG

Tel. +44 (0) 1635 24 88 33
Fax. +44 (0) 1635 24 85 95
info@papadakis.net
www.papadakis.net

Editorial and design director: Alexandra Papadakis
Editor: Sheila de Vallée
Editorial Assistant: Sarah Roberts
Designer: Vicky Cardin
Design Assistant: Hayley Williams

ISBN 978 1901092 790

Copyright © 2009 Sue Eden and Papadakis Publisher
All rights reserved
Sue Eden hereby asserts her moral right to be identified as author of this work.

No part of this publication may be reproduced or transmitted in any form or by any means, electronic or mechanical, including photocopy, recording or any other information storage and retrieval system, without prior permission in writing from the Publisher.

Printed and bound in China

Contents

- 7 Foreword
- 11 Introduction

THE COMMON DORMOUSE
- 17
- 20 The elusive dormouse
- 22 Distribution of dormice in Britain
- 27 What does the dormouse eat?
- 32 Habitats used by dormice
- 42 Movement and dispersal of dormice
- 43 Conservation management for dormice
- 46 Dormouse nests
- 50 Hibernation
- 55 Summer torpor
- 57 Breeding in dormice
- 59 Predation of dormice

SURVEYING FOR DORMICE
- 65
- 66 Searching for hazel nuts eaten by dormice
- 68 Searching for dormouse nests
- 70 Providing artificial nesting sites for dormice

OTHER STUDIES ON DORMICE IN BRITAIN
- 82
- 84 A Mad Hatter's tea party?
- 85 The Nut Hunts: finding the distribution of dormice in Britain
- 87 Nest Boxes and the National Dormouse Monitoring Programme
- 88 Nesting tubes
- 89 The numbers game
- 92 Breeding potential of dormice
- 93 Food
- 94 Habitat
- 96 Dispersal of dormice: sink or source populations?
- 99 Conservation action for dormice

CONCLUSIONS
- 108

APPENDIX
- 111
- 111 My own experiences of monitoring dormice
- 112 Kingcombe Meadows Reserve
- 116 Our garden
- 119 West Bexington Reserve
- 122 Ryewater Nursery
- 125 Abbotsbury Swannery
- 126 Bibliography
- 127 Footnotes
- 128 Postscript
- 128 Acknowledgements

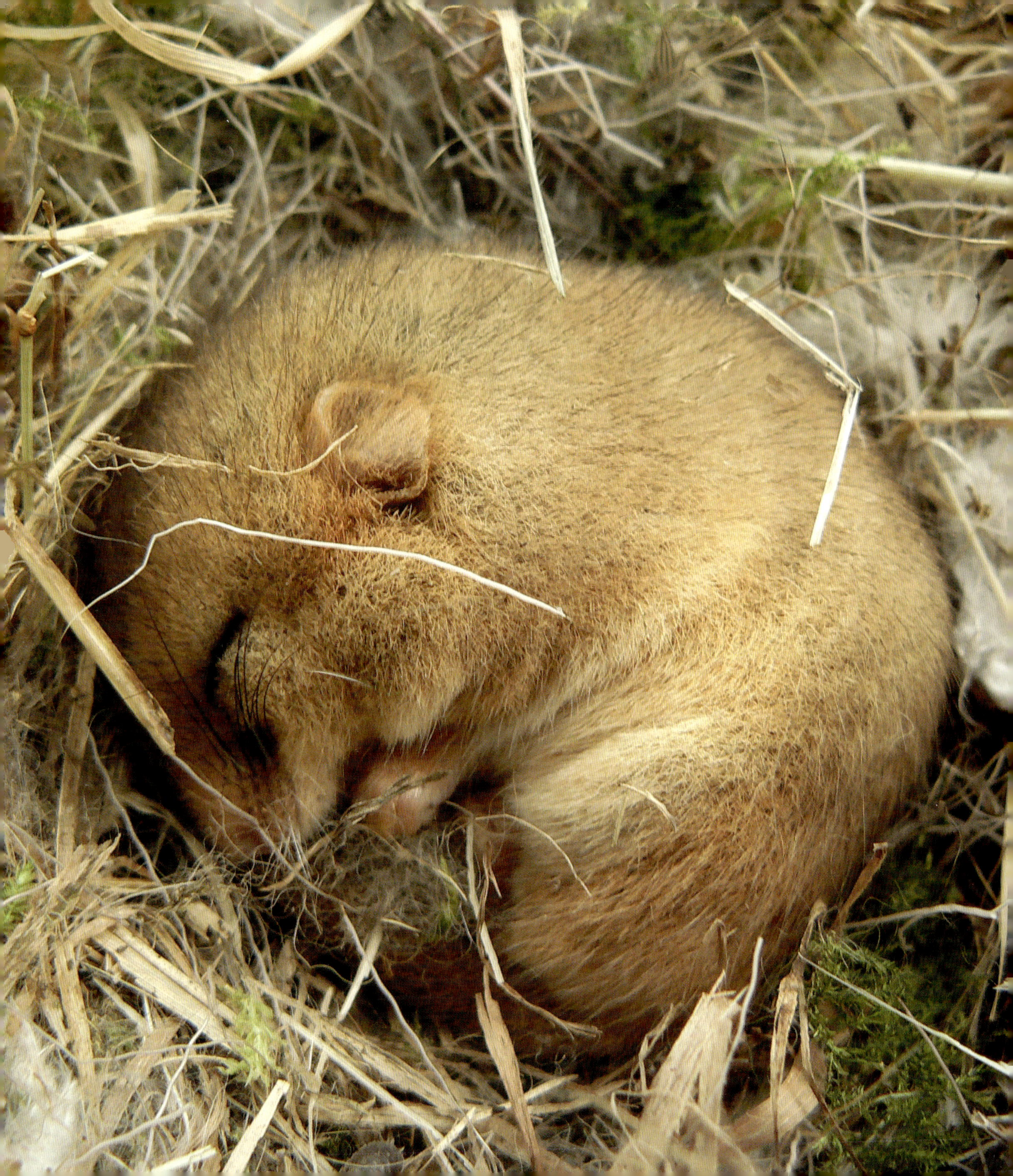

Foreword
by Professor Perrins

As an ornithologist, I have always found dormice rather confusing little creatures. I first met dormice as a schoolboy helping with a survey of nesting tits in boxes at Alice Holt on the Surrey/Sussex border. There, especially in the conifer plantations, we used to find them curled up asleep in the nest-boxes – and I am sure with a smile on their faces – amidst the empty eggshells. It didn't seem quite the right sort of place, as my mammal guides said things like "frequents mature deciduous woodland, needs hazel."

I moved to Oxford where for most of my working life I carried out fieldwork in Wytham Woods, which should be ideal habitat for dormice, with plenty of hazel, but they are not there. Sue Eden makes the point that they are extremely elusive and easily missed, but in Wytham generations of pellet-searching students have shown that not even the much-studied Tawny Owls can find them.

It was in Oxford that I first met Roy Eden, where he was a veterinary surgeon. I later met up with Roy and Sue down in Dorset where they had retired, as I was studying the swans at Abbotsbury. There they re-introduced me to dormice. Not only had they found dormice at The Swannery, but they found them in good numbers in their 'garden' of blackthorn scrub and bramble, and in the scrub along the coast, not a woodland or a hazel in sight, clearly not where they are supposed to be.

In this book Sue explains how finding dormice living in these 'wrong' habitats has enabled her to gain a better understanding of dormice in general. She has found that they must rely on a different range of foods from the specialist flower and fruit diet previously said to be essential. She suggests that the importance of insects has been previously grossly under-estimated, and relates a report of a captive animal that ate its way through a hundred and forty-nine privet hawk moth caterpillars in a single night.

She has found dormice to be an almost universal denizen of all arboreal habitats in the southern counties where she has worked, but the true distribution of dormice in the Midlands and further north still must be worked out, the Oxford area included! It is hoped that this book will inspire others to go and seek for signs of dormice. Sue has found that the previously assumed rarity of dormice can be attributed to the survey methods used. For instance the extreme fickleness in dormouse occupation of nest boxes can make box surveys of them unreliable. Box use may also be related to competition with, or at least interference from, the more numerous wood mouse.

No one will be able to read this fascinating study without coming away both wiser and with a sneaking respect for the sturdy little animal – a true but elusive survivor.

Professor Christopher Perrins

above: Professor Christopher Perrins meeting a dormouse in our garden

opposite: A dormouse asleep in a tit's nest with a smug look on his face – was it scrambled eggs for breakfast?

The Common Dormouse

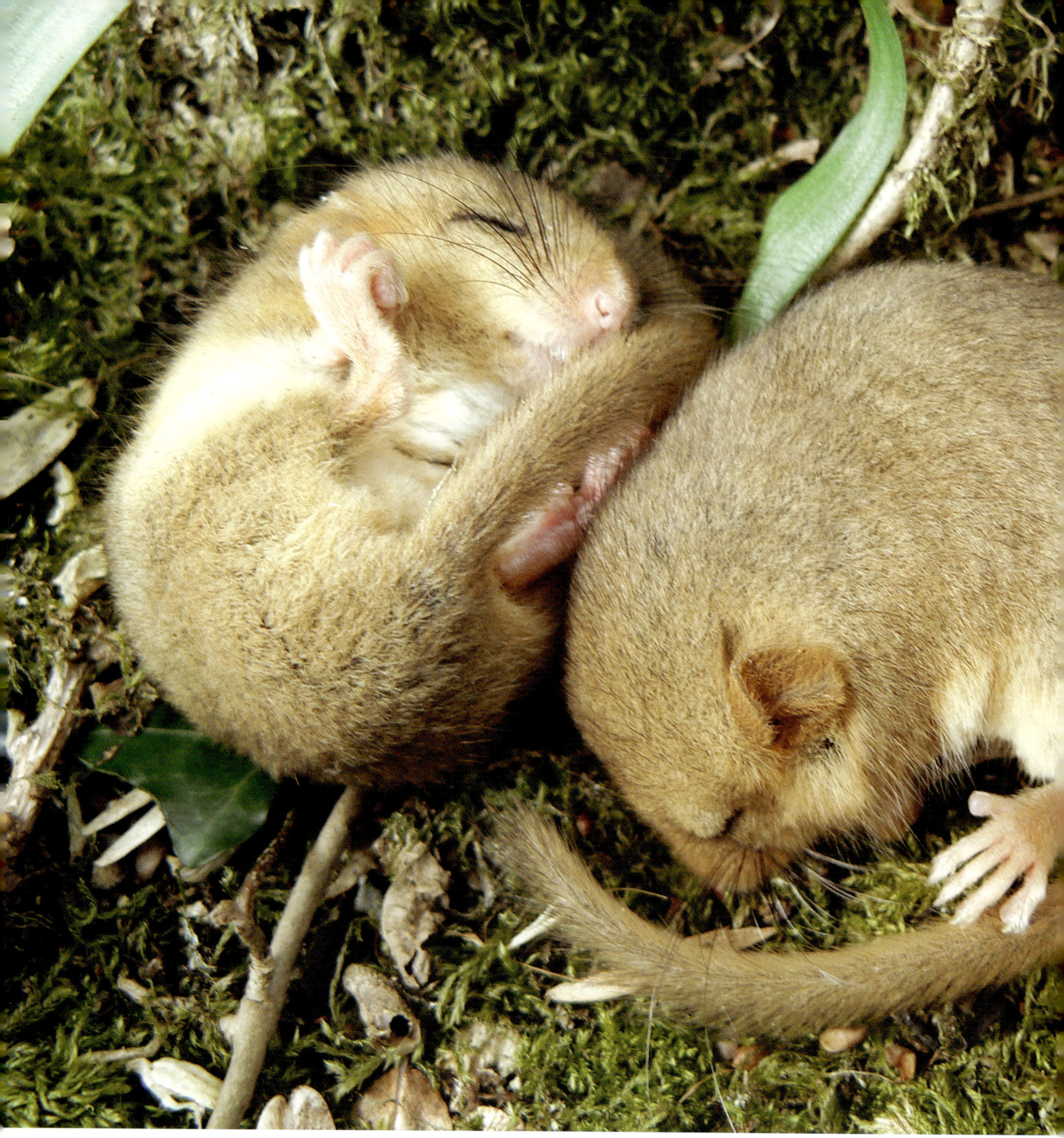

Living with
dormice

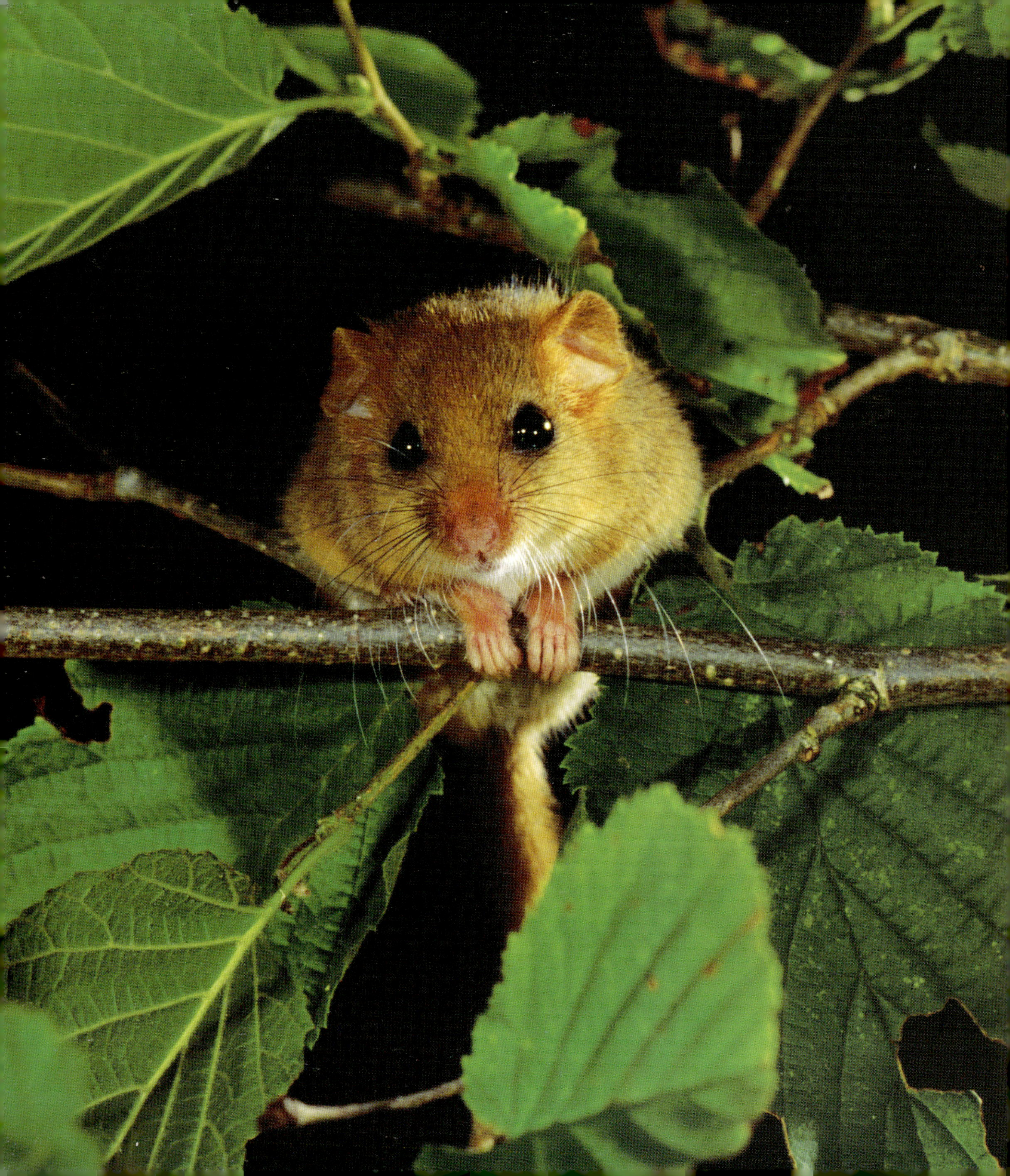

Real rodent or phantom of the ancient wood?

The common dormouse is said to be a very rare animal, usually found only in ancient woodland, with not only the right species of trees and shrubs to provide its special food needs, but requiring interventionist management to produce just the right conditions for it to survive. But here they were in our garden, a patch of coastal blackthorn scrub far from any woodland.

Intrigued by this anomaly I started investigating. Gradually over the years – the dormouse being the most elusive of creatures and rarely seen – I have found that it is in fact a widespread opportunistic omnivore; a tough little tree mouse, well capable of finding enough food to fatten up for hibernation in the storm-battered branches of species poor coastal scrub, far from any woodland, and remote from the hazel nuts with which it is associated in most people's minds.

Much has been written about dormice in Britain over the last twenty years, and several books published only very recently. Almost all previously published work in Britain, on which laws and conservation action for dormice are based, has originated from the conclusions drawn from a limited source of research, carried out only in what was thought to be "best" habitat. It might seem superfluous to produce yet another publication, but my own work on dormice in other habitats has uncovered a very different dormouse from that written about previously. I have for the past eighteen years lived where there are dormice in the garden, and after years of browsing through the countryside of Dorset, I now realise that dormice are widespread and plentiful, and anything but a rare animal. Here they appear just as at home in low coastal scrub and in conifer plantations as they do in any ancient deciduous woodland.

I have always had a general interest in small mammals, but studied botany, and then went on to do botanical research. I was working as a marine ecologist when I met my husband Roy, a veterinary surgeon. When he retired in 1988 I longed to get back to the coast and we moved to Dorset, to a bungalow behind the Chesil Bank.

That I would actually meet a dormouse had never entered my head – was it not a very rare animal of ancient woods, never likely to be seen? Like most people my only acquaintance with a dormouse came from reading Lewis Carroll's *Alice's Adventures in Wonderland*, where I had mistakenly learnt that it was a largish mouse that sleeps in teapots. Well, how was one expected to know that the dormouse had been at the magic mushroom, and that in reality it is only about the size of an ordinary mouse?

Soon after we moved to Dorset, we were lucky enough to acquire an extension to our garden in the form of a patch of coastal scrub, about one third of a hectare in size, on which the developer had been unable to build. The scrub looked rather uninteresting: a salt-blasted, impenetrable area of blackthorn with some bramble and wild privet, about a hundred metres from the sea. It was recent scrub that had been grassland some twenty years previously. While my husband was trying to fence the area he disturbed a small pile of old cut grass and

previous page: A pair of dormice in summer torpor

above: Most people think of a dormouse as the sleepy creature from *Alice's Adventures in Wonderland*

opposite: The dormouse is an arboreal rodent – most at home among the branches where it hunts for its food

The Common Dormouse

above: Blackthorn scrub on the hillside above the village of West Bexington, West Dorset. Habitat in which dormice are widespread

discovered two dormice hibernating underneath. My first dormice: and a dormouse curled up asleep in torpor with its tail over its nose is not easily forgotten! As some literature states, "You've only got to take one look and you're hooked," or "Stare a dormouse in the whiskers and you're lost." Little did I know when I looked upon my first dormouse that it was the start of many years of struggling in and out of bramble patches, spiny blackthorn bushes and getting hooked up on barbed wire. How much simpler it would have been if I had kept to the books and studied dormice in hazel coppice woodland.

Hooked by this intriguing animal I wanted to find out more. Fortunately in 1992, Doug Woods, a naturalist from Somerset, was giving an adult education day locally on dormice. It was Doug who had found that dormice would use wooden nest boxes, and thus made studies of them seem feasible. The study day leaflet stated that "any person who wishes to know more about these animals will find these days rewarding and possibly the start of a continuing interest." Well, all these years later I am still trying to learn about dormice, a credit indeed to Doug's teaching and enthusiasm. Roy and I went on a further course and then obtained licences so we could put up nest boxes and handle any dormice that we found. I wanted to know what they were doing in our garden, having subsequently read that they needed large woods for populations to stay viable, and that they needed woods with fruiting hazel. Our garden was far from any woods, and hazel was absent, as it is extremely sensitive to salt. Roy set to making boxes and has been an invaluable aid in the practical management of our various nest box schemes. We have carried out the fieldwork together.

My knowledge of dormice has been gradually gained over years of browsing and observing. What I have been doing might be called natural history by some but it is the basic understanding of the lifestyle of an animal that is needed. As well as carrying out

12 *Living with Dormice*

some general surveys, I have studied dormice for more than twelve years by means of artificial nesting sites in various habitats across Dorset. I now feel I can explain the seeming anomaly of our first dormice and that I have sufficient evidence to challenge the generally accepted status quo of the dormouse.

I hope that this book will be helpful to those already monitoring dormice, but also to anyone who would like to start looking for signs of them, as well as people just interested in knowing more about British wildlife in general. I present my findings to encourage others to report their experiences of these most elusive of small mammals, to think flexibly when working with dormice, and not be surprised at what they find.

Although I touch on most aspects of their biology, I do not intend this to be a comprehensive book on dormice. I have concentrated on my own experiences and observations; needless to say there is still much to be discovered about their distribution, abundance and biology. My findings have major implications on dormouse conservation and on the management of the habitat in which dormice occur.

I shall begin by covering aspects of the biology of the dormouse based mainly on my own observations and on discussions with others who have been monitoring dormice. I am grateful to members of the Dorset Dormouse Group and to others across Britain, especially Gordon Vaughan of Okehampton, who have shown me their nest box schemes and discussed their work with me. Through their work I have been able to see the range of woodlands where dormice are to be found, and in particular how abundant they can be in high forest and conifer plantations. However, it is doubtful if I would ever have realised just how adaptable and widespread they are, had I not come to live right by the sea, in an area where the arboreal habitat consists mostly of patches of species poor scrub and hedgerows often blasted by salt-laden winds. It was finding how common they are in such an extreme habitat that led me to conclude that the dormouse is not the animal previously described.

I have tried most of the main ways of surveying for the presence of dormice, and found serious flaws in them. Other researchers have relied on these methods, and I believe it is this that has led to ideas of dormouse rarity. Later on I discuss these methods and include some of my own results, which I hope will help explain how I have reached my conclusions. More details of my results are given in the Appendix. The dormouse is very elusive, and will probably always be a challenge for researchers, but this means that all casual observations can add to our knowledge of this appealing animal.

Aerial view of the village of West Bexington. The wild part of our garden is part of the blackthorn scrub behind the beach huts. There are records of dormice from nine other gardens in the village

a dormouse curled up asleep in torpor with its tail over its nose is not easily forgotten!'

The Common Dormouse 13

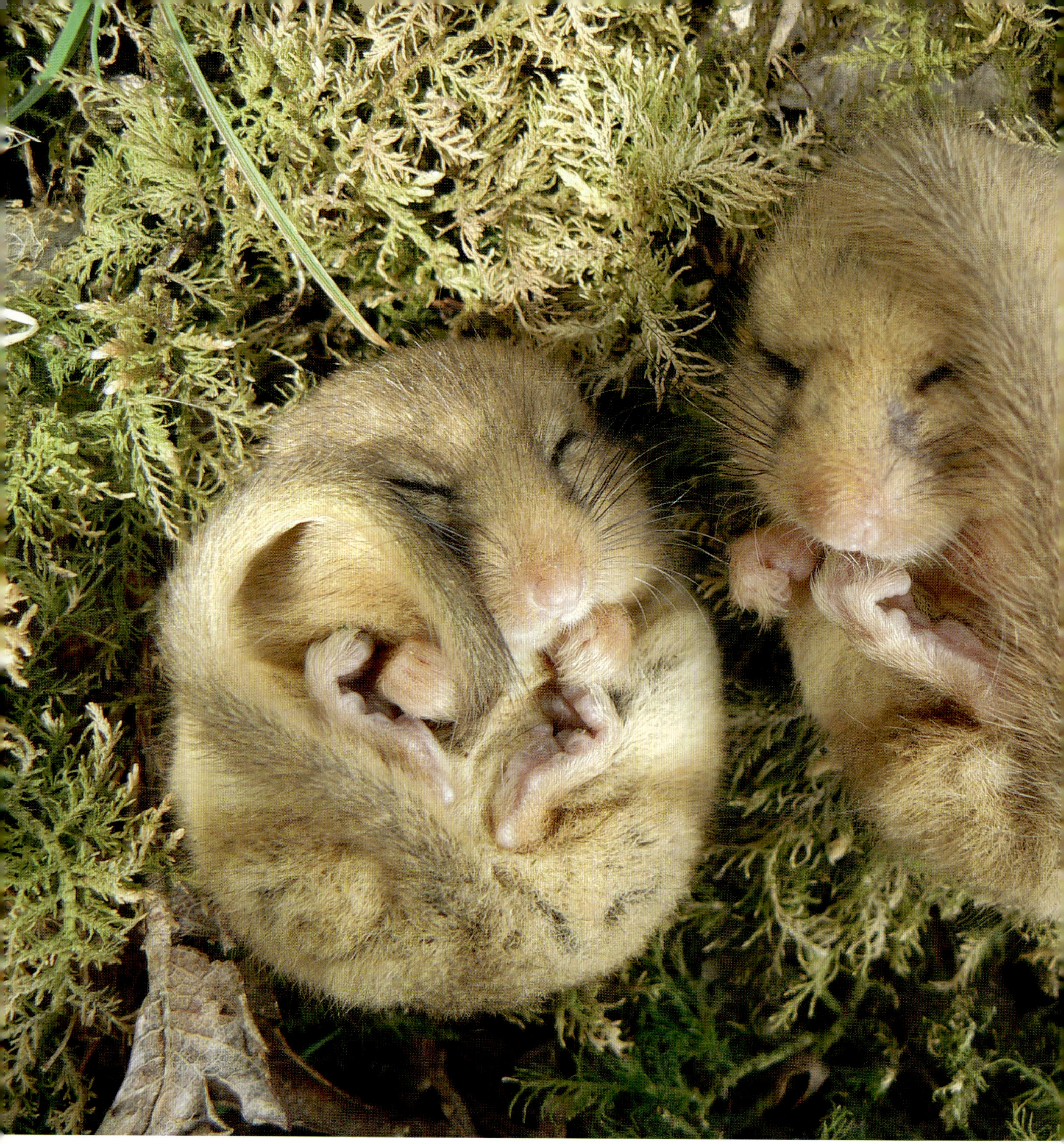

The common dormouse

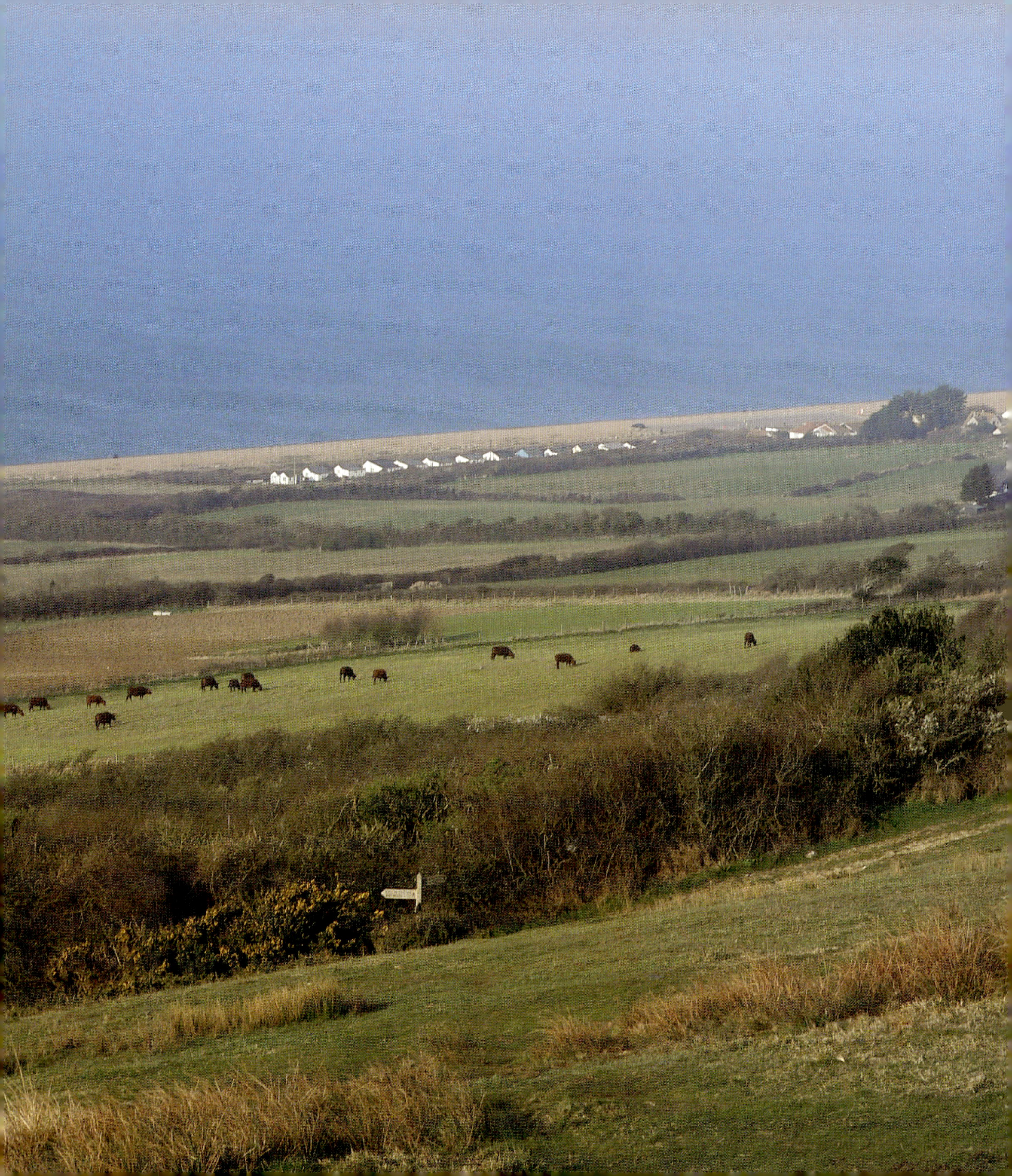

The common dormouse (*Muscardinus avellanarius*), often referred to as the hazel dormouse, is the only native species of dormouse that occurs in Britain. Dormice are rodents, but belong to a small, distinctive family, the Gliridae. Several species of dormice occur in Europe. The edible dormouse (*Glis glis*), a much larger animal than the common dormouse, was introduced into Britain at the beginning of the twentieth century and is still largely restricted to the Chilterns but scattered records of it occur from other areas, including Dorset. In appearance it is rather like a small grey squirrel; it can cause serious damage to trees and enters houses in large numbers, where it can create havoc. The subject of this book is the common dormouse, referred to as just "the dormouse." It is widespread on the Continent, where it occurs from the southern Baltic to southern France, and also parts of the Mediterranean, including Sicily and Corfu. In the east it occurs in European Russia and northern Asia Minor. The limits of its north-westerly range are in Britain. There are no reports of it causing damage like its larger relative, the edible dormouse.

Dormice are the only small rodents to have furry tails. Other distinctive characters of the dormouse family are that they have a different dentition, having four molar teeth instead of the usual three in rodents, and the crowns of the teeth are traversed by a series of parallel ridges. Also they lack a caecum, the part of the digestive system that aids digestion of green leaves in other mammals. There are over twenty-five species of dormice, half of which occur in Africa and the others from Western Europe to Japan.

The dormouse is much the same size but more compact and rounded in shape than the wood mouse (*Apodemus sylvaticus*). Its body is some 6-9cm long with a tail slightly shorter than its body. Many people, including professional ecologists, find that it is much smaller than they expected. This is doubtless due to the many larger than life-size pictures of it, and partly to the illustrations of it at the Mad Hatter's Tea Party in Lewis Carroll's *Alice's Adventures in Wonderland*, where it was rather too large to be stuffed into a teapot. During its active season the dormouse is usually somewhere between 15-20 grams, but in preparation for hibernation it is usually nearer 30 grams, and can occasionally reach over 40 grams. It is said to be easily distinguishable from other British mice by its long furry tail and attractive gingery coloured fur. The chest is paler and there is usually a creamy white patch on the throat. The descriptions given of the colour of a dormouse range from gingery to bright golden, to sandy or orangey-brown. But whatever the colour is called, it can be somewhat misleading as it is only the adults that are such a lovely colour. I have seen incredulous looks on people's faces when shown their first dormouse in the form of a small, grey youngster, not the much larger animal that they

previous page: Dormice just beginning to wake up from summer torpor. The male is the larger animal on the right. The female was probably born later and is not quite fully grown

above: Dormice are only the same size as ordinary mice. This drawing is probably largely to blame for making people think they are much bigger

opposite: View of the lower part of West Bexington from the hill above, showing some of the hedges and scrub where many dormouse nests have been found

the name 'dormouse' is thought to be derived from the French 'dormir' to sleep

The Common Dormouse 17

expected to see with bright ginger fur and a bushy tail. Descriptions often say the tail is bushy, but it is in no way like the tail of a squirrel, and thickly furry is a better description. Dormice have neat rounded ears and a blunt nose with very long whiskers and prominent black eyes. The fore limbs are relatively short and the feet are prehensile, so that they can turn out at almost right angles to enable it to grip branches firmly. The feet have pads on them to assist in grasping branches, and the fore feet have only four digits, the thumbs being reduced to stumps, an adaptation found in other tree-climbing mammals, such as squirrels.

The dormouse is the only British rodent that truly hibernates; when in torpor its body temperature falls to near that of its surroundings and all bodily functions are reduced to a minimum, so that it is in a state where it needs very little energy to stay alive. The dormouse can also go into torpor for shorter periods at other times of the year. When in torpor it has an endearing way of curling up with its tail over its nose, and in this position it is likely to be identified with confidence by any novice, as it can so easily be handled and looked at. Without experience, few people would be confident at identifying it on a quick glimpse of an active dormouse disappearing into the bushes.

The dormouse is one of our best-loved mammals, but few people have ever seen one. It is generally held to be just the dozy animal at the Mad Hatter's tea party, and a mere

above: A field mouse – a fierce competitor of the dormouse. Note the large ears and almost naked tail

top: An adult dormouse in torpor, with gingery fur, a well furred tail and long whiskers

18   *Living with Dormice*

phantom of the ancient wood, so rare that it is never likely to be seen. Dormice are not really rare, but are such elusive little animals that seeing one is most likely to be a chance event. Much of their elusiveness is because they generally feed high up in trees and bushes at night time, they hibernate for up to half the year, and live at lower densities than other small rodents. The name "dormouse" is thought to be derived from the French *dormir* (to sleep), after their habit of going into torpor when hibernating in winter, but also for parts of the day at other times of the year. There are numerous local names, one of the most widespread being the "seven-sleeper."

The dormouse is a very charismatic little animal: it is often said to be the most beautiful and captivating of British wild animals. Bill Oddie even said in one of his television programmes, "If there is a prettier little animal in the world I have yet to see it." The dormouse has become one of the chief icons of British wildlife. It is thought to be so special and so rare, that there always seems to be kudos in being able to claim it as present on any nature reserve. Most people consider seeing a dormouse a very memorable occasion. In letters of thanks after I have shown them to people, I have received such comments as: "It was a very special experience." "A great privilege." "We were really spellbound by the whole experience."

Images of dormice are frequently used in all sorts of literature, more so than almost any other British mammal. Rarely can one open a magazine on wildlife, without seeing a picture of one. It is frequently used for adverts for Wildlife Trusts, for holidays and courses, even at degree level in conservation and land management. Its cuteness has often been exploited in procuring funds, even taking the form of Adopt-a-Dormouse schemes. Many photographers seem to aim at getting images of dormice into their portfolios, and occasionally such images are demeaning for what should surely be pictured as a truly wild animal. Dormice are most often shown curled up in torpor, but it is never mentioned that they usually have to be turned over on their backs for this unnatural, but most endearing pose. The most demeaning example of photographic "art" I have come across was of a row of curled up young dormice placed in the upturned trumpets of daffodils, like eggs in eggcups. Its cuteness has led to much misplaced attention being thrust upon it.

The dormouse is a protected animal: it is illegal to disturb, kill or injure, capture or possess a dormouse or to damage or destroy its nesting places. To study dormice and consequently handle and disturb them it is necessary to have a licence from the appropriate Statutory Nature Conservation Organisation. Regulations require developers to carry out surveys and implement mitigation measures if dormice are displaced by their activities.

Laws to protect the dormouse were enacted because, although not immediately endangered at the national level, it was thought to be rare and to be threatened by contraction of distribution and numbers as a result of progressive local extinctions. The dormouse was given partial legal protection under the Wildlife & Countryside Act 1981, and a later amendment in 1988 made it a fully protected species. In 1994 it was made a European protected species. It is now a priority species in the UK Biodiversity Action Plan, which commits the Government to restoring its range, by appropriate habitat management and reintroductions.

A pair of dormice in summer torpor showing the position they usually rest in. The fur of the one on the left is more adult in colouring than the greyer youngster on the right

Springtime. A dormouse in torpor in a tube before building a nest, illustrating the position in which they usually rest

The elusive dormouse

If there is one word that should be applied to dormice, it is elusive. Dormice are very rarely seen, even when searched for. They are most often found by people working in the countryside, who are carrying out management, such as coppicing in woodland, and they are not likely to report the sighting.

It is relatively easy to find out which birds there are in any area, but small mammals are largely nocturnal and rarely seen, except when trapped or brought in by the cat. The dormouse is probably more elusive than most because it lives in relatively low densities, leading an arboreal lifestyle up in the branches of trees and shrubs, and hibernates for up to half the year. Dormice are rarely caught in traps.

For many years it has been said that dormice have a strict dependence on woodland, so this is the only habitat where most people actively look for them. Woodland can be one of the hardest places in which to detect them as illustrated by what happened in Savernake Forest, ancient woodland of over a thousand hectares in Wiltshire: dormouse eaten hazelnuts were found in 1993, but the first record of a live dormouse was not until 2004, when one was found in a bat box.[1]

Surveying for dormice is usually carried out by searching for signs left by them, in the form of eaten hazel nuts and the characteristic nests that they build. The easiest way to see dormice is by putting up artificial nest sites, usually in the form of nest boxes or nest tubes. That people have concluded that dormice are rare is largely due to the reliance put on these methods, which need to be used with caution and which can produce too many negative results. I have tried to understand why such methods can be useful at times, but can so often fail. This will be discussed in detail later, with some of my own results as illustrations of their limitations.

Most sightings of dormice in the wild are purely by chance, and give little indication of their true distribution or abundance. They are so elusive that although they are often seen in "strange" places, any one person would be very lucky to ever stumble across one unless he or she were actively managing dormouse habitat. However, the possibility of someone seeing a dormouse partly depends not only on the work they do in the countryside, but also on both their awareness and perception of what is around them. A local hedge-layer, who loves dormice, says he regularly finds dormice in the hedges where he is working, and a local thatcher seems to consider finding a dormouse up in a thatch quite a normal occurrence. In contrast, I know of a farm in West Dorset, still with the same appearance that it would have had a hundred years ago, consisting of small fields surrounded by tall hedges, where a friend checked with nesting tubes, and

in Victorian times dormice were often kept as pets

Living with Dormice

found dormice to be common. However, the farmer, who was born there over sixty years ago, did not know they were there. The farmers in our own village, although they are very perceptive and able to recognise rare grasses from a tractor cab were also unaware that there were dormice on their farm. They have brought me two dormice since they were made aware of their presence: one from among bales they were moving and one brought in by their cat. It is surprising how easily dormice can be overlooked.

Now that most operations in the countryside, such as hedge management, have been mechanised, even fewer people are likely to come across a dormouse. An illustration often cited to prove that dormice were common in the Victorian age was of children taking them to school in their pockets. But lifestyles have changed and unfortunately today's children are far more sedentary. How many children today explore local habitats, and even if they do live in the countryside ever walk to school? That said on questioning villagers in country areas of Dorset, I have found that several recall having seen a dormouse, usually in torpor, rolled up with its hairy tail over its nose, so the reports can be accepted as trustworthy.

Many country people do not know about sending in records, or even that county record offices exist. In the Victorian era, when there were few means of transport, the local naturalist, often the local clergyman, would have known and talked to the local woodsmen and hedge layers, who were the people who would have seen most dormice. The perceived greater abundance of dormice in the Victorian era is derived from such comments from woodsmen as dormice are "frequently found" and "so common," but some workers in the Dorset countryside still make similar comments. Nowadays there seem to be more distractions in people's lives. Committed naturalists are thin on the ground, and their role has in many ways been usurped by the professional, whose knowledge comes more out of books, and who spend more time staring at computer screens than delving into hedges. Perhaps it is not surprising that most of the present day records of dormice that are sent into the Dorset Environmental Records Centre come from gardens. In Victorian times dormice were often kept as pets, so many more people would have seen one and have been able to recognise one, whereas today most people have never seen one.

Since my first accidental sighting of a dormouse, I have stumbled across very few in the wild. From using nest boxes I know that they are numerous in the wild part of our garden, but I have only twice seen them there except in the artificial nesting sites. The first was when my husband, Roy, was using a brush cutter and disturbed a hibernation nest. On the other occasion I found one drowned in a water butt in the vegetable garden, which I did not even recognise as a dormouse until it was dry! In all the years of exploring good dormouse areas in Dorset I have stumbled across only six more: four in nests and two while helping coppice in woodland. Because of my known interest, I have been shown three hibernating dormice and been brought several casualties or corpses.

most sightings of dormice in the wild are purely by chance, and give little indication of their true abundance

opposite and below: Dormice are not always asleep. When checking dormouse boxes they are often found in torpor in the Spring. This gives an opportunity for some quick photography before putting them back in the boxes. When awake, dormice are far too quick and nimble to photograph in the wild

The Common Dormouse

Distribution of dormice in Britain

In Victorian times the dormouse was a familiar animal to country folk, and even described as abundantly found in many districts of England.[1] Today it is seldom recorded but no one seems sure whether it is rare and threatened or merely overlooked. Recent articles state that it is one of Britain's rarest animals and declining over most of its range. The present day distribution in England is given as only patchy but widespread across the southern counties, from Kent to Cornwall, and in the Welsh border counties, much rarer in the Midlands and eastern counties, but absent north of a line from south Norfolk to Cheshire, except for a very few sites known in Cumbria and Northumberland. In Wales dormice are said to be very scattered, mainly occurring near the English border. It is generally said that there are none in Scotland, but it does appear that there have been a few early records as far north as Glasgow.[2] The first national dormouse survey concluded that dormice had probably become extinct in seven counties during the last hundred years.[3] This finding is said to be confirmed by later surveys.

If people are told that dormice are rare and unlikely to be seen, they do not feel encouraged to look for them. By way of its lifestyle, the dormouse is a very secretive animal, and even when flourishing can give the false impression of being rare, or even absent. So in many ways it is not the easiest animal to study. However, most records of dormouse absence or extinction are based on insufficient exploration. I know of too many cases where it has taken several years to prove the presence of dormice.

From my survey results and the work of other people in Dorset, I do not find dormice to be patchily distributed, but to be widespread. They seem to occur in virtually any reasonable arboreal habitat. Indeed, they are no more restricted to woodland than are wood mice. There seems no reason why dormice should not be found in all types of arboreal habitats, and be widespread over much of Britain, at least where they have been found in the past. Even modern agricultural practices do not appear to have been radical enough to eradicate them where a network of hedges has survived.

With the increased interest in dormice, records are now progressively appearing from counties where dormice were previously held to be extinct. For example, dormice have been found again in Staffordshire;[4] and in Warwickshire six sites have recently been found, spread widely across the county.[5] Dormice were thought to be rare in the Midlands because of the medieval open pastures, but they obviously remained in some woodlands, and should have had time to move into the hedgerows. It would be harder to detect them there because of the relative scarcity of hazel compared with southern hedges. No one without some experience will find a dormouse nest in a hedgerow and confidently record it as such; and even if they did find a nest, the record would probably be rejected, as the dormouse is now held to be extremely rare and confined mostly to woodland. In Shropshire

In the Spring, pairs of dormice can be found in nest boxes. But the males take no part in building the breeding nests or bringing up the family

22 *Living with Dormice*

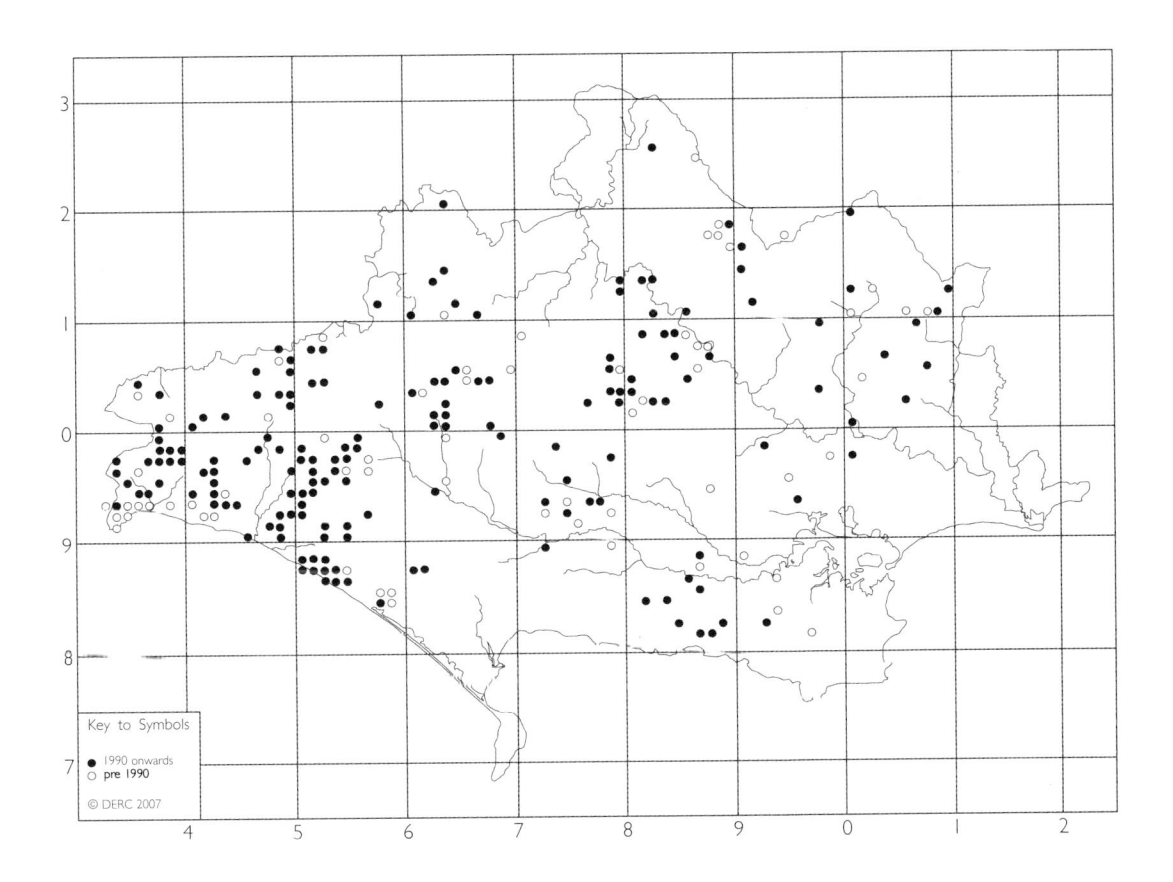

dormice are now known to be present in over fifty sites,[6] whereas in 1925 a report stated that they seemed to have disappeared from Shropshire, as none had been seen for three or four years. Such vacillations in the perceived status of the dormouse are not new; even before the First World War, reports stated that the dormouse was becoming rare in many areas, long before any decrease could be blamed on the impact of modern land management.

Dormouse populations appear more scattered in the north of England, thought now to be their northerly limit within Britain. The more southerly distribution of dormice mimics that of several insectivores; it may be that such animals need a longer feeding season and drier conditions than those usually prevalent in the north. Although dormice appear to be rare in the north, it seems that they have not become extinct over such large areas as suggested, and may be grossly under-recorded. Only about four sites are now recorded from the north of England, whereas in Victorian times more than twenty-five sites were recorded. Even in the most northern areas dormice have been found in such habitat as gorse scrub,[7] and in woodland that is predominantly coniferous, habitats not previously considered as suitable for dormice even in the south of the country. It certainly seems possible that dormice are able to live in many more northerly sites, on the basis of some of the local climates where they are found further south. Dormice flourish in the relatively wet, cold woodlands on the northern slopes of Dartmoor,[8] and have been found at an altitude of 400m in the Brecon Beacons National Park.[9] The atrociously wet summer of 2007 in no way appeared to have deterred dormice breeding in Dorset. In July most of the males ought to have been in summer torpor but the females were active with broods of young.

Distribution of dormice in Dorset based on records received by the Dorset Environmental Records Centre. The map was produced by DERC using DMAP software. The greater abundance in the west of the county is merely due to my having carried out more searches in this area

A dormice positioned to show off its long whiskers – an adaptation which is helpful when moving among branches in the dark

The dormouse appears to be grossly under recorded over all its range in Britain. When I first started looking for evidence of dormice, I was modifying the dormouse distribution map in Dorset at a fast pace. Before 1990 dormice had been recorded from some 59 kilometre squares. In the following ten years with increased interest and my surveys, 134 more records for kilometre squares were added, hardly the indicator of a rare animal. Now alas I find my impetus diminished; they are just too common and there are family pressures – and groans, "Not looking for those things again!" Although I have scaled down my searches for new sites, I still find that in winter I can usually find signs of dormice in most areas I visit in the county.

Recent surveys of deciduous woods in Kent of over 10 hectares revealed the almost universal presence of dormice. The surveyors were surprised that dormice were also found in an isolated wood of only one hectare. They queried whether this meant that Kent was therefore the flagship county in England for dormice, or just that Kent had been more extensively surveyed than other counties.[10] I would suggest that Kent is still under surveyed and it will be interesting to see what happens if searches move from woodland to habitats down to the size of hedgerows and bramble patches.

I disagree with the conclusions, made after the first national dormouse survey that there seem to be no areas where dormice can be said to "commonly occur."[13] I have found that they are common in the woods and in the hedgerows of the pastoral areas of Dorset, and I see no reason why this should not be the case over most of the southern counties. I have to agree

Living with Dormice

though that dormice cannot be "easily found" unless artificial nesting sites are provided, but even these can fail in years where there is competition with other small rodents. Lack of recent records where dormice have previously been found should in no way be taken as proof of extinction. There is as yet no universally workable method of detecting their presence. I find it impossible to guess the true densities at which dormice live but I believe it to be much greater than previous estimations. This problem will be discussed in greater detail later.

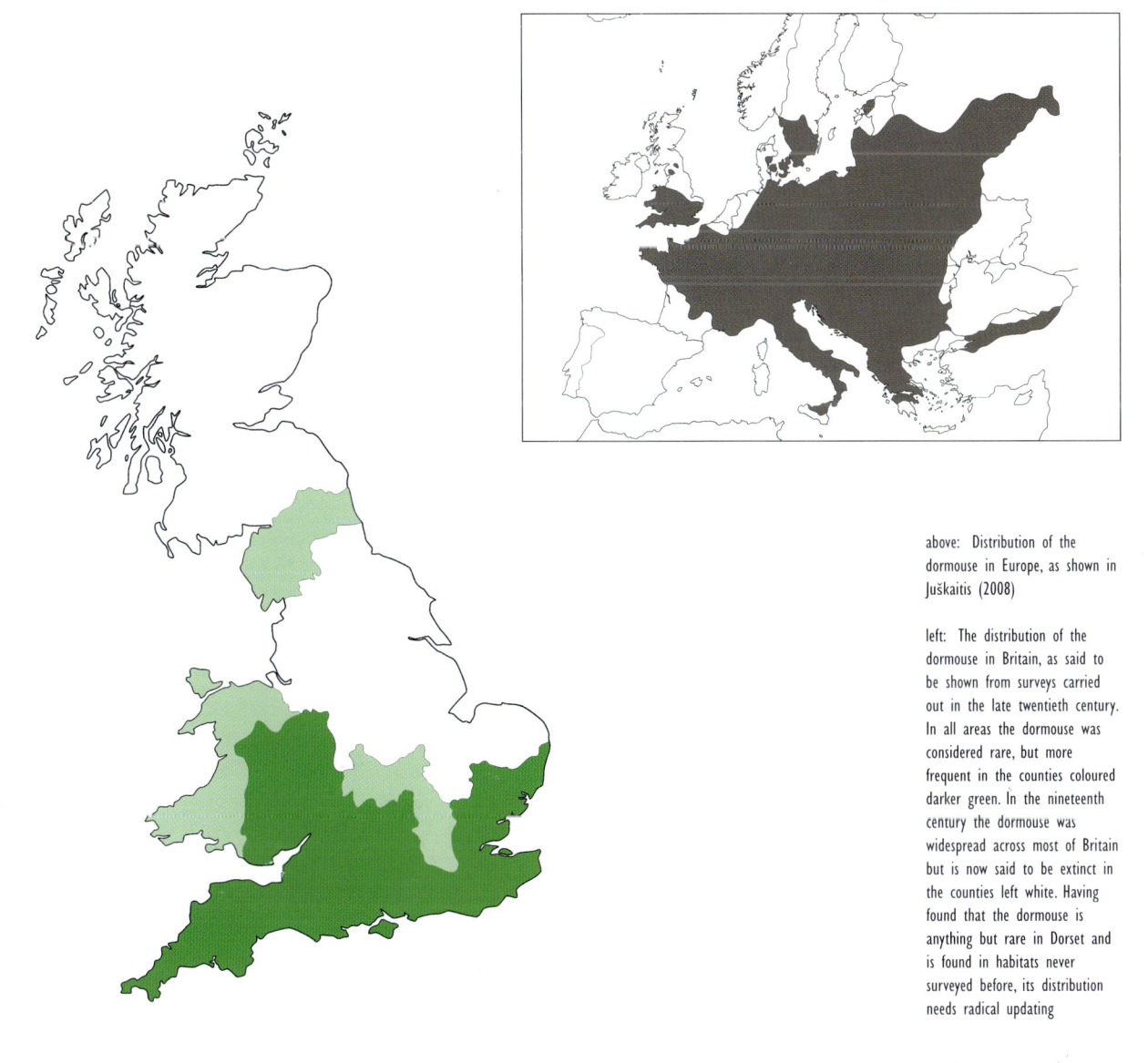

above: Distribution of the dormouse in Europe, as shown in Juškaitis (2008)

left: The distribution of the dormouse in Britain, as said to be shown from surveys carried out in the late twentieth century. In all areas the dormouse was considered rare, but more frequent in the counties coloured darker green. In the nineteenth century the dormouse was widespread across most of Britain but is now said to be extinct in the counties left white. Having found that the dormouse is anything but rare in Dorset and is found in habitats never surveyed before, its distribution needs radical updating

The Common Dormouse   25

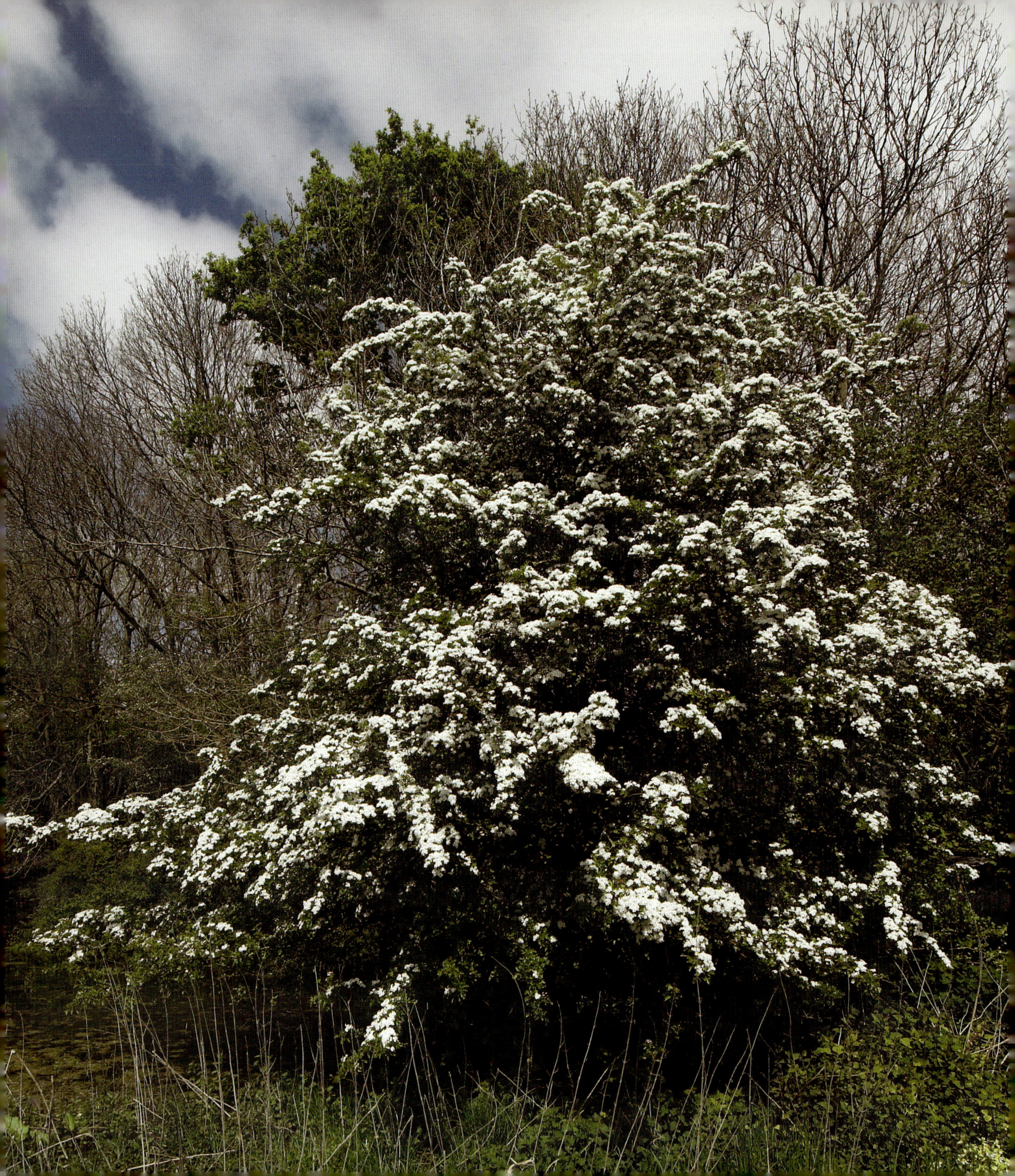

What does the dormouse eat?

The dormouse is a versatile omnivore able to adapt its diet to its surroundings in a wide range of habitats. The principal foods that it eats are flowers, fruits, nuts and insects. It differs anatomically from other rodents in that it does not have a caecum, so is unable to live on green vegetable matter and has to rely on higher-grade food. It does though at times supplement its diet with more digestible young leaves and with buds.

The dormouse feeds mainly up in the branches of trees and shrubs. When they are in flower or fruit, dormice target them as they provide an easy source of food. Flowers from a wide range of species have been recorded as eaten by dormice, including the catkins of hazel and oak, the flowers of hawthorn and other rosaceous tree species, and the male cones of conifers. Pollen is said to be an important food source, but as the walls of mature pollen are very resistant to digestion and nearly all pollen found in faecal pellets of dormice is still intact, this is dubious. It is probably significant that dormice tend to choose younger flowers, and it is from the other parts of the flower, such as the nectaries of honeysuckle flowers, that they gain more nutrients.[1] Certain species have been held to be especially important as food plants, the most important being hazel, oak, honeysuckle and bramble. It is even said that no good habitat lacks two or more of these species. However, dormice are now being found to be plentiful in habitats lacking these species. As well as eating the flowers and seeds of trees and shrubs, dormice have been recorded coming down and feeding on such herbaceous species as ramsons, willowherb and greater wood rush.

Hazelnuts have long been considered an important food for dormice and their principal source of food before hibernation. Contrary to such widespread beliefs, from the habitats in which I find dormice, it is obvious that hazel is certainly not an essential food. It is unfortunate that the dormouse is often called the hazel dormouse, as this reinforces the idea of an inextricable link. Most hazel starts ripening in late August, a good month or more before most dormice fatten up for hibernation, and grey squirrels have often demolished most of the crop long before the nuts are ripe. Some of the best breeding and over wintering successes I recorded were in 1995, in an area where the hazel produced no nuts as a result of a severe drought. In some years I have found that the male dormice seem to fatten up while hazelnuts are available, but many females are still rearing young long after this. It can take as long as twenty minutes for a dormouse to open and get all the contents out of a hazel nut, so it may be that nuts are not always the most efficient food source. It is probable that the rich insect fauna associated with hazel is of greater value to dormice than the nuts, which are only available for a very short time each year.

There seems to be no evidence that dormice utilise acorns or fill nest boxes with acorns, as yellow-necked mice (*Apodemus flavicollis*) do. In captivity dormice never take more than a trial

above: With fruits such as sloes, the dormouse is after the kernels, the most nutritious part of the fruit

opposite: Hawthorn bush in flower. Dormice appear to be very partial to such flowers. It may not be just the flowers that they are eating, though, as insects are abundant around flowers too

Oak trees provide a good source of insects for dormice, especially in the Spring when there are hoards of caterpillars

insects are one of the most important of foods for dormice

nibble at an acorn, presumably the tannin content is too high for them. It is more likely that their predilection for insects rather than acorns explains why they are often found feeding in oak trees.

Previous findings state that dormice struggle to find enough food and have to supplement their diet with insects in mid summer, as food is scarce when the tree flowers are over and fruits not yet ripe. But it does seem that insects are one of the most important of foods for dormice. In many habitats where dormice live, insects must of necessity form an important constituent of the dormouse's food for much of the year, in view of the absence of flowers or fruit for most of the dormouse's active season. Mid summer, when flowers and fruit are in short supply in woodland, is the time when insect populations peak and it often coincides with a peak in dormouse breeding.

The dormouse's predilection for insects has been demonstrated by some radio tracking studies. An earlier study found that in one wood, early in the year, the dormice were spending most of their time up in oak trees, where there would be a plentiful supply of caterpillars, but by June they spent more time among the shrub layer feeding on aphids and caterpillars.[2] Another study showed that dormice were devouring hoards of insects and visiting trees, which were without flowers or fruits. Their faecal pellets showed that insects could account for up to 80 per cent of their food in June.[3] Reports of dormice, kept as pets early last century, have also shown their partiality for insects as food. There is a report of one pet dormouse that escaped and consumed 149 "fine" privet hawk moth caterpillars in a single night.[4] Edward Step, in his book *Animal Life of the British Isles* (1921), describes how his pet dormice were fond of climbing the curtains and hunting for flies.

Living with Dormice

Dormice seem to have a very catholic taste in insects and have been described hanging by their hind legs from the leaves of sycamore, vacuuming up hundreds of aphids.[3] I found that an injured dormouse, which we had in for treatment, would consume a dozen macro moths a night, even when provided with a surplus of blackberries and shelled sunflower seed. Dormice have been seen running around a moth trap, catching moths on the ground, and there are reports of others found actually in moth traps.[5] I am suspicious of the motives of the dormice in the wild part of our garden, as twice I have found nests within feet of where Roy runs a moth trap almost every night!

Dormice eat other animal food such as birds' eggs, although there seems to be no evidence that they purposely seek out such food. On several occasions I have found them in boxes nesting under a bird's nest that contains eaten eggs. They have been found to eat numerous eggs of the pied flycatcher in nest boxes in woods on the fringes of Dartmoor.[6] On the Continent there have been assertions that dormice eat young birds and even adult birds, but other workers have not verified this in extensive surveys. Rather they have occasionally found dormice pecked to death by great tits.[7]

In the coastal scrub where much of my work with dormice has been undertaken I have learnt much about their versatility and omnivorous appetites. The scrub is mainly composed of blackthorn with some patches of brambles. There are few if any other shrub species producing flowers and fruit that could provide food for the dormice. Some places where I regularly find dormouse nests are so close to the sea that they are in areas where few blackberries develop and the blackthorn rarely flowers. In such coastal areas dormice come out of hibernation around the beginning of April when the blackthorn is in flower but then there are few flowers of any sort until June, when a late flowering species of bramble, which is the dominant bramble of the area, starts to flower. Bramble has generally been held to be a key source of food for dormice, as it is in flower or fruit for most of the season. I first thought bramble must be of particular importance in the coastal scrub, but I have since changed my mind. I now consider insects of much greater importance to dormice than previously realised.[8] In our garden one June, I found a dormouse with well grown young before any of the brambles were in flower. The whole growth of the young must have taken place without any arboreal flowers as food. Perhaps more significantly, on several occasions I have recorded dormice fattening up for hibernation long after all the blackberries had gone. It is notable that dormice on an inland site readily used boxes in recently laid hedges, before even the brambles produced any flowers and fruit.

It is still a puzzle as to what the dormice in the coastal scrub do eat to fatten up before hibernation. Whatever it is, it must be very nutritious, as they can double their weight in as little as ten days. There are sloes, but some years these are rare. Both dormice and wood mice eat sloes, but neither is interested in the tart flesh around the stone; what they are after is the more nutritious seed inside the stone. But these would barely seem adequate as their main food source in autumn. It would be very hard work for a dormouse to open enough sloes to enable such rapid weight gain. One winter I had in a very young, underweight youngster, who for a long time would eat nothing but sloes, as if they constituted the only food he had ever been shown

Privet hawk moth. Dormice are very partial to moths and have even been found in moth traps

Hawk moth caterpillar. A captive dormouse was once recorded to have eaten 149 'fine' privet hawk moth caterpillars in a single night!

by his mother. He was opening up to twenty-five sloe stones a night, and ignoring all the other food that he was offered. It was not until, in desperation, I tried him on digestive biscuits (a food suggested by Doug Woods) that at last his weight started to shoot up – lovers of digestive biscuits beware! I still feel that insects must be an important food for dormice, but they are often fattening up for hibernation so late that one would think that there could not be enough insects still around.

In laboratory experimentation to find what dormice will eat, the Cruelty to Animals Act prescribes that captive animals are always supplied with suitable food that they are used to. The animals tested are usually laboratory bred, so when supplied with food that they usually eat, they are most likely to eat that, and not show what other foods they could eat in the wild. A couple of times I have taken in injured dormice, and occasionally underweight youngsters, after the winter has set in and they have little hope of surviving. These have always been returned to the place where they were found, when fit to do so. I always give them food such as sunflower seed, which I know dormice like, but it is food that they have not encountered before. At the same time I give them a selection of food available in the wild. Among my more interesting observations was proof of their voracious appetite for such insects as moths. When given blackberries, they usually open each pip to get at the seeds, which are presumably more nutritious than the flesh. Dormice from the coastal scrub are unused to hazel nuts and it takes several days – sorry nights – before they realise that the nuts are edible. On one occasion, two very young dormice ate every bud off the twigs they were given to climb, just leaving the brown outer scales. Is this a possible food source in the wild? In the spring, even when supplied with plenty of nuts, dormice will eat young leaves. They seem particularly fond of honeysuckle leaves, but also like leaves of hawthorn and most other rosaceous shrubs, and are quite keen on the shoots of garden peas. Even from the few observations that I have made, I find that they are very individualistic in their food preferences. One dormouse would eat up every scrap of digestive biscuit in preference to other foods, while another, who was obviously frantic for food and cleared almost everything offered it, when given a piece of biscuit pushed it to one side to get at the sunflower seed underneath.

Other rodents in woodland have generally been studied at ground level, and their arboreal behaviour neglected. It has been suggested that dormice, by feeding more in the canopy, achieve enough vertical separation from other species to sufficiently reduce competition for food.[1] This is debatable: in low scrub and hedgerows this is often not the case. It seems that dormice must often compete in exactly the same habitat for the same foods as the more numerous wood mice. Perhaps in some habitats in the early part of the year, dormice specialise in eating flowers and nectar more than wood mice, but for most of the year both are generalist feeders, eating seeds, fruits and insects.

top: Sloe stones opened by dormice. Note the round holes with smooth edges

above: Sloe stones opened by wood mice. Note the more angular edges to the hole and teeth marks at right angles to it

opposite: Hedgerow leading down to the sea. Here the dormice usually nest in the patches of wild madder

Living with Dormice

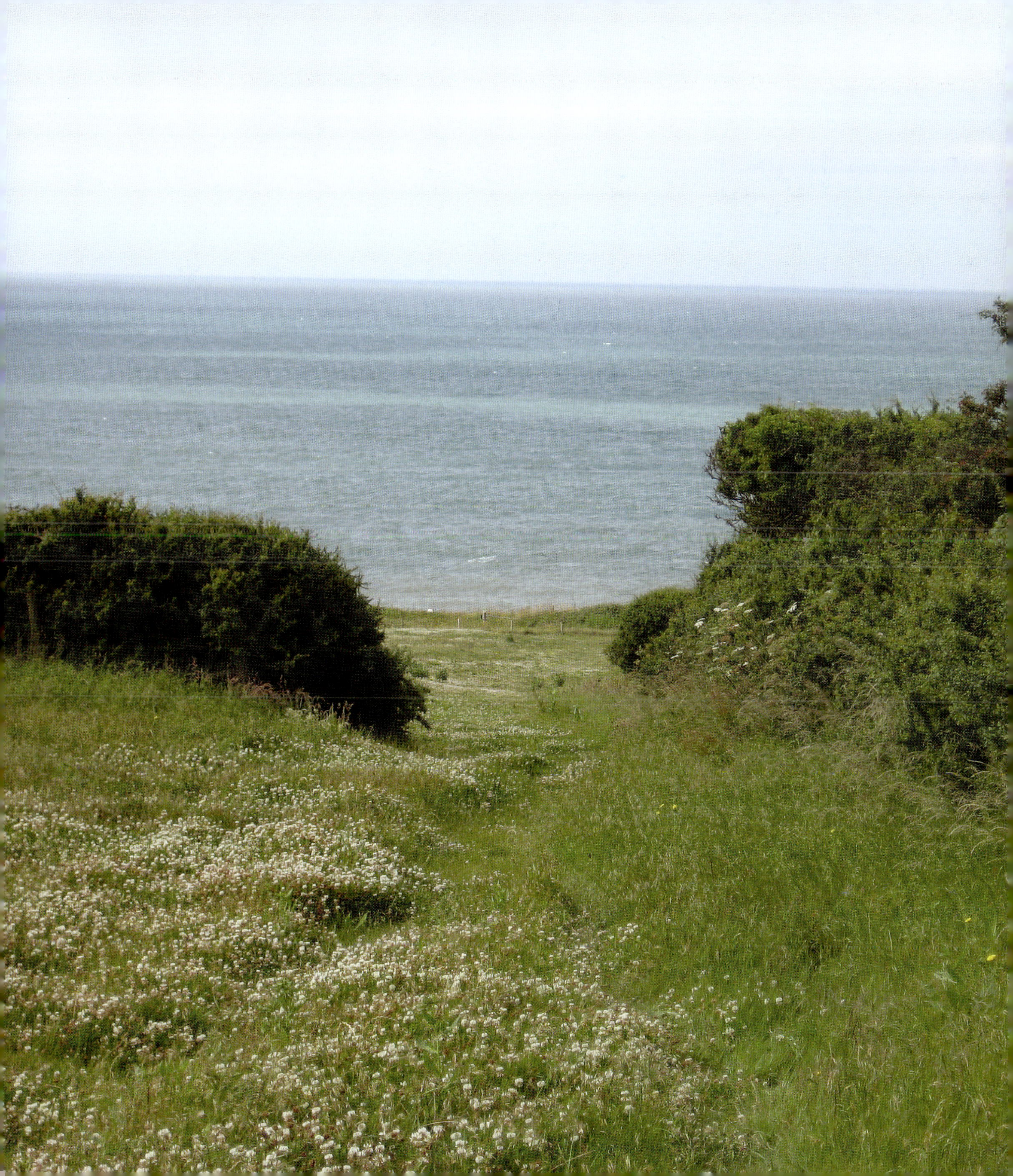

Habitats used by dormice

below: Patch of low scrub just above Chesil Beach, where dormice occur. The scrub is separated from inland scrub by a trackway

bottom: Low salt-sculpted hedge, abutting the Chesil Bank, where dormice nests have been found

Entrenched in the mind of many people, professional ecologists and land managers included, is the idea that dormice are rare animals only to be found in hazel coppice in ancient woodland. Even the advice given by Frances Pitt early last century for finding a dormouse, as it "seeks honeysuckle bark for its nests and nuts for its fare," was to look in hazel coppice, "where the hazel bushes grow thickly beneath the trees, their twigs laced together by honeysuckle ropes, the acrobat of the bushes has its headquarters."[1] She had found dormice "in tall, old, gone-wild hedges" but says that this was "exceptional and the proper place to look for it is beneath the trees."

The dormouse is an arboreal rodent, that is it hunts for most of its food and lives, during its active season in the branches of bushes and shrubs. Despite previous ideas as to where to hunt for dormice, it is actually to be found thriving in nearly all types of arboreal habitat from low bramble patches to large forests of mature trees with little if any understorey. The dormouse lives among nearly all species of trees and shrubs including conifers, particularly where the species produces good crops of flowers and fruits or has abundant insect populations. Dormice use habitats as variable as areas of almost pure gorse or blackthorn scrub, to mixed oak woodland, to conifer plantation over all its range in Britain. They also use other non-woody vegetation that is strong enough to provide a framework in which to climb, and hunt for food in such habitats as reed beds. They also come down to the ground for some foods such as the flowers or seeds of herbaceous plants.

It was only by chance that we discovered dormice living in the coastal blackthorn scrub in the wild part of our garden in a habitat that has none of the characteristics previously said to be essential for them. Having found dormice as abundant here as recorded in "good" woodland, I started looking for signs of dormice in all arboreal habitats in Dorset. They were once said to be the very symbol of woodland life and to be excellent indicators of the health and sustainability of a wood. In reality I find that dormice inhabit almost any arboreal habitat, and cannot be held to indicate any particularly special quality of the habitat, except perhaps that there is a good insect population associated with the vegetation.

You may be thinking that I found plenty of dormice in Dorset because dormice are relatively abundant in the southern counties. But dormice have previously been considered rare animals with only a patchy distribution, dependent mainly on large ancient woodlands. West Dorset, where I have carried out most of my work, is one of the most sparsely wooded areas in southern Britain, and the woods here are generally rather small. I have concentrated on habitats other than woodland. What I have found here is relevant over all the range of the dormouse. Indeed, there are increasingly reports from all over England and Wales of dormice being found in non-woodland sites.

I have concentrated on what up to now have been called "exceptional" places. In fact, such places should be accepted as perfectly normal. The hazelnut and nest searches that I carried out in Dorset showed that dormice often occur in hedgerows and patches of scrub many miles distant from any woodland.[2] In the coastal scrub and hedges I have found dormouse nests scattered throughout the area, where there are often no arboreal linkages even to the few larger patches of scrub. Evidence of dormice in so many places and in all types of arboreal habitat has led me to consider dormice as normal universal occupants of virtually any arboreal habitat, but very elusive ones. My confidence in such a radical conclusion is bolstered by the fact that I have found evidence of dormice in extremes of arboreal habitat, most notably in low salt sculpted blackthorn and bramble actually on the beach of the Chesil Bank. I have found dormouse nests easier to find in these locations than in classically "good" woods, and dormouse eaten hazel nuts easier to find in locations away from woods.

The range of habitats in which I have seen evidence of dormice is corroborated by the results of the South West Dormouse Project.[3] One of its main aims was to discover whether records of dormice in "odd" places away from traditional habitats of woodlands and hedgerows were just aberrations or could be repeated. Nest tubes were used for this survey, and although tubes were not found to be a universal panacea for finding dormice, they did show that dormice were in such habitats as coastal scrub on the Lizard in Cornwall, in managed as well as unmanaged hedgerows, in species poor hedges and scrub and in areas of almost pure gorse, many distant from any woodland.

above: View from Shipton Hill, West Dorset. Only a few small woods exist, but dormice are widespread in the hedgerows

below: Hazel coppice woodland. Habitat that previously was thought to be essential for dormice

The Common Dormouse

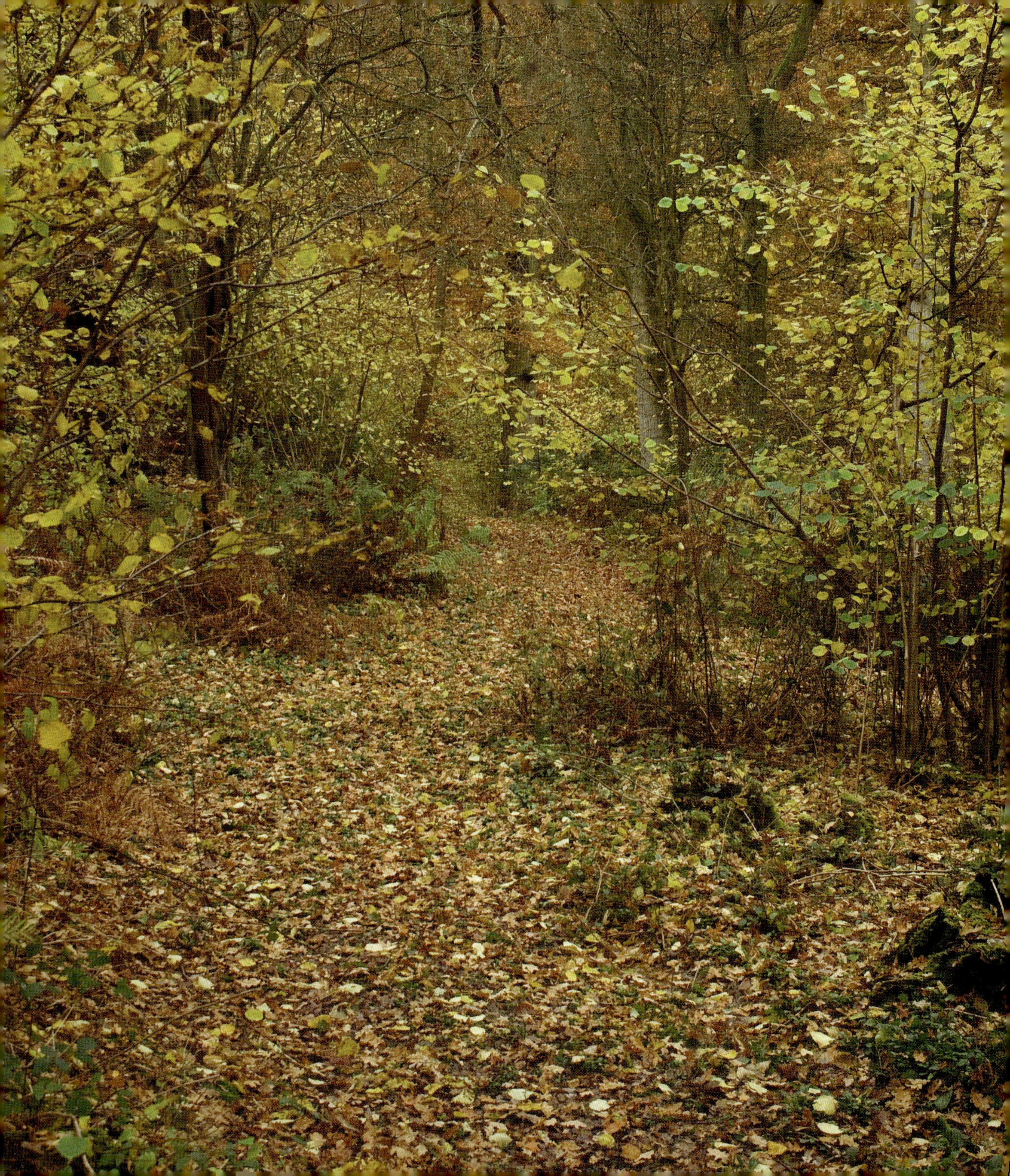

Deciduous woodland

Dormice appear to thrive in nearly all types of broadleaf, deciduous woodland. The only possible exception may be where an area has become dominated by species that form poor habitats for insect life, such as dense areas of ash saplings. It has been said that they do not like woods shaded by too many standard trees, but the canopy of high forest has not been properly studied and has been generally dismissed as of little use to dormice. There is always a sunlit area in any woodland even if it is at the tops of the trees, and here insect and plant food can be found. The positioning of boxes is important when trying to attract dormice and they seem more attracted to boxes that are in the leafy, feeding zone of vegetation. Boxes placed only 1-2m up tree trunks, well below the leafy zone – and especially where there is no ground vegetation with which to weave nests – are more than likely to be ignored. In high forest, comprising mainly standard trees, it is often bat boxes placed high up in the trees that are successful in attracting dormice.

The canopy of high forest increases the dormouse's elusiveness, except to the few stalwarts willing to use ladders. Gordon Vaughan was such an intrepid worker in oak woodland, on the northern slopes of Dartmoor near Okehampton, Devon. He was able to show that such high forest can hold abundant dormice.[1] Here some of the woods have a high canopy of oak with almost nothing below but a few scattered holly bushes, and no shrubby borders. He put up nest boxes for pied flycatchers some 3-5m above ground level, and this produced far better numbers of dormice than have been recorded in most coppiced woodland. By putting up bird boxes Gordon reckoned not only had he attracted the largest colony of pied flycatchers in southern England but also the largest known colony of dormice in south-west England. The weather in the woods on the slopes of Dartmoor, especially the high rainfall, would seem unsuitable for dormice. Gordon said, "If dormice can live and breed successfully in these conditions then they can do it in many other places." When I had the pleasure of going round the woods with him the way he found dormice in box after box seemed like magic.

Gordon's work has shown that the branching system of mature trees can provide as good an arboreal habitat for dormice as do shrubs. In Hungary dormice have similarly been found to use the canopy layer of young pure hornbeam forests, some 15-20m above ground level. Shrubby areas provide good arboreal structure for dormice at a height most easily observed by humans, whereas high forest may provide just as good a maze of horizontal pathways through a mass of trees, but away from the gaze of most mortals. High forest is one of the hardest habitats in which to prove the presence of dormice. Fruiting hazel is virtually absent, so no evidence from eaten nuts; there is little undergrowth in which to find nests; and any nest boxes probably need to be placed high up near the canopy. Patience is also needed; in one wood it was eleven years before the dormice started to use Gordon's nest boxes.

> it is often bat boxes placed high up in the trees that are successful in attracting dormice

above: High Oak woodland at Okehampton with Gordon Vaughan checking nest boxes high on the trunks of trees. Note the lack of shrub layer

opposite: Deciduous woodland with a good understorey of shrubs. Excellent habitat for dormice – but so are many other habitats

The Common Dormouse

Coniferous woods

opposite: In the Spring a pair or a male and two female dormice can be found together. At this time of year they are often in torpor for part of the day

below: Staward Gorge, Northumberland, the most northerly known site in England. Dormice were first found here in an area of dense conifers

Dormice are found in conifer plantations, and seem very at home there. Initially it was thought that these were merely relict populations in ancient woods that had been planted up with conifers. However, they seem to be as abundant in areas where the conifers have been planted on heathland in Dorset as in sites where conifers were planted to replace deciduous woodland. It would therefore seem that not only is it possible for them to live in conifers, but that conifers produce good habitat for them.

This is confirmed by the fact that such habitat is where dormice are found in some of the most northerly of their locations. In the most northerly known site in England, in Northumberland, the woodland is composed of 60 per cent conifers, and the dormice were first found in an area where conifers are dominant. They also occur in conifer-dominated areas in Sweden, the most northerly known locations in Europe. I have been shown areas of conifer plantation where dormice, from box occupation, seemed more abundant than in hazel coppice. These sites were in areas where there was no ground flora and no arboreal access to any adjacent alternative habitat. Equally, I have seen good numbers of dormice in areas of conifers where they could have moved easily to adjacent deciduous woodland. Although dormice do build nests in conifers, often in the angles where the branches meet the trunks and needles collect, it appears that nest boxes on conifers are at times more readily chosen than those in some other habitats. Dormice appear to use plantations of a wide range of conifer species.

It is not yet known what foods the dormice are utilising in the conifers. Some conifers support high densities of aphids, but the dormice may be exploiting buds and sap as well as insect food, male cones and seeds. It may be that the density of insects in some conifers is the important factor, and the shelter of the evergreens may provide a crop of insects that is available for a longer part of the year than would be the case in deciduous woodland. It is significant that some bats choose to feed in conifer plantations rather than in adjacent deciduous woodland, and seem to find them a particularly valuable hunting ground in late autumn.

Coniferisation of ancient woodlands has not done as much harm to dormouse populations as previously thought. In the past, in some places clear felling of conifers took place for the sake of dormice. This just removes good dormouse habitat, without being able to offer a good alternative for many years, and is disastrous to many other animals. We need to know more about the species that live and depend on conifers; the present fashion for clearing conifers to produce open heathland may be detrimental in some areas to rare animals such as some bat species.

above: Conifer plantation in Wyre Forest. The dormice seem to favour this area rather than moving into the surrounding deciduous woodland

Living with Dormice

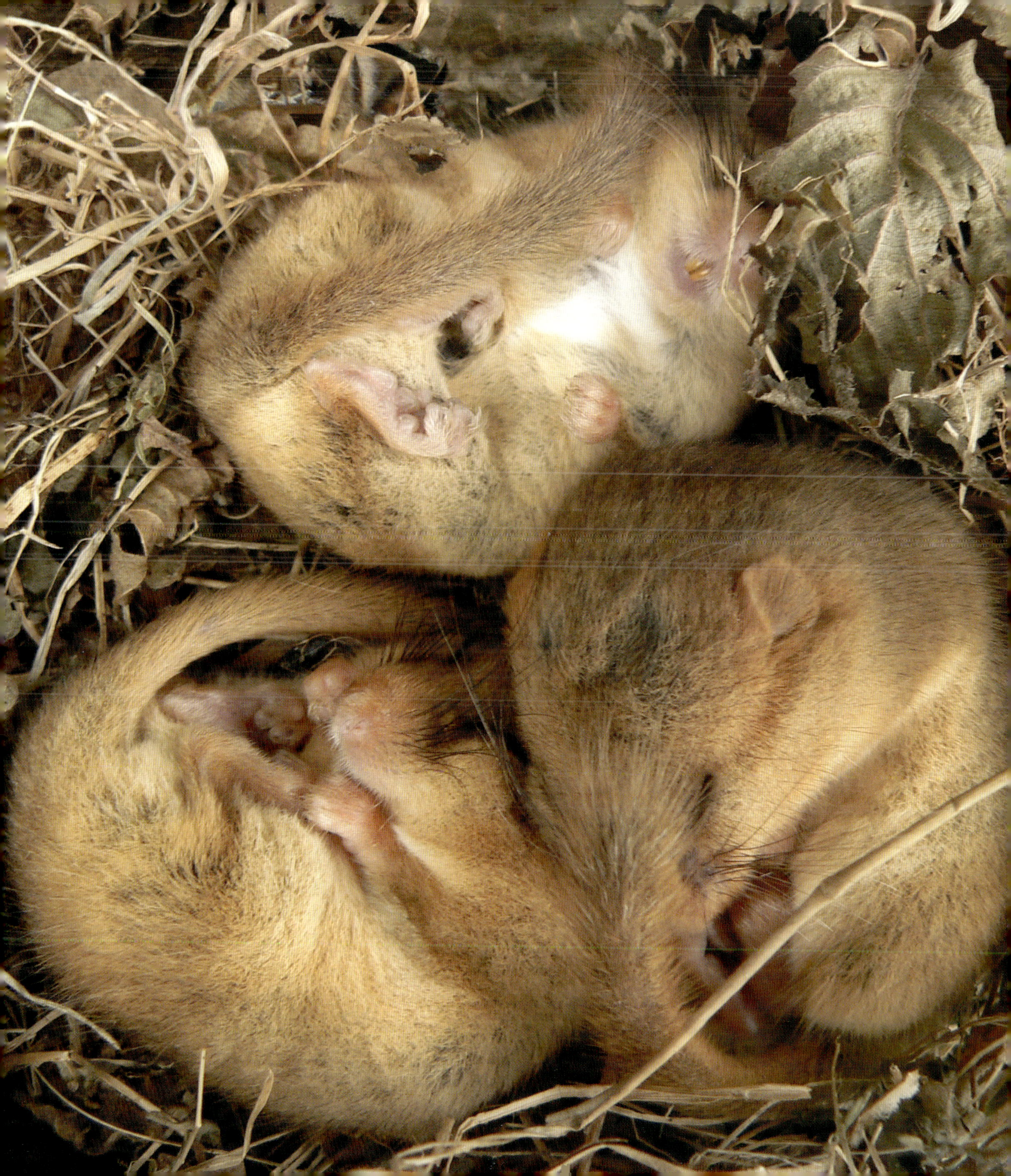

Scrub

Many of the bushes that form scrub produce abundant flowers and fruits, but also support a large number of insects. Just what dormice need. Even blackthorn supports about 150 species of insects, with hawthorn and willow supporting even more. Unfortunately for the dormouse in most agricultural areas, even if hedgerows remain, all scrub has been removed. Where scrub does remain, it is often deemed to be wasteland, and many use it to dump rubbish. We have removed all sorts, from refrigerators to cookers, from our patch of coastal scrub, and it is an ongoing problem. Few eulogise about scrub. When the last patch of scrub fronting the road in our village was cleared for building, the adjacent neighbour was pleased, and said that a nice house would improve the whole road. Even ecologists rarely have anything good to say about scrub, with most not even considering it a proper habitat, just transitional vegetation between open grassland and woodland. To the conservationist it is the enemy of grassland, seemingly to be cleared at all costs. This is a pity, as so many areas of scrub have been lost in Britain, before we have had time to ascertain their true ecological value.

Dormice have been found in a wide range of scrub type habitats, many of them made up of few species. I have found nests in areas of bramble and in areas of almost pure blackthorn in coastal scrub. I have been shown a dormouse nest built in a nest tube in an area of several hectares of almost pure gorse, where the nest material included many gorse needles! Dormice have been recorded nesting in gorse patches as far north as Cumbria.[1] When looking for dormice, the advice has always been to avoid wet areas, especially those that might seasonally flood. However, I have found them associated with blackthorn scrub invading a reed bed. They have also been recorded in willow carr and reed beds around Slapton Ley in Devon. In South Wales two dormice were trapped some 50m out into a reed bed adjoining a willow carr, to the surprise of the surveyors who were looking for harvest mice.[2] Dormice have also been found associated with the scrub and hedges of the wet culm grassland areas of Devon, and in willow scrub in Cornwall.

It seems that dormice utilize almost any type of scrub vegetation, or indeed any vegetation in which they can climb about to find food. I have not heard of them using any agricultural crops in Britain, but a friend recounts having seen one climbing around in a crop of maize in France.

above: Large area of gorse on the Lulworth Ranges, South Dorset. The presence of dormice was discovered using nest tubes

top: Coastal scrub where dormouse nests have been found. The scrub is mainly composed of blackthorn, with some bramble

Living with Dormice

Hedges

Dormice appear to be almost universal denizens of most hedgerows in Dorset. I have found nests in hedgerows far from woods, in ones where there are few woody species, and in ones that are cut back each year and produce almost no flowers and fruits. From my observations they seem to use hedgerows as they would any other arboreal habitat, and in no way should any hedges be considered primarily as dispersal routes.

Dormice were commonly encountered in hedgerows in the nineteenth century, when the cutting was done by hand and the workmen would have found the dormice. Similarly, I know of a local hedge layer who still often finds dormice. The hedges in my home area on the coast are seldom mechanically cut, as they are kept in shape by the salt winds; this tends to mean that there are more structures in which they are likely to anchor nests where they can be found easily. From nest evidence here, dormice are widespread, even though most of the hedges are species poor and usually produce little fruit. The actual dispersal of dormice over the area is uncertain, but nests are very widely dispersed, suggesting a universal occupation of the hedges and scrub. I am still astounded at the extremes of arboreal habitat that dormice will use in this coastal area. In some places just behind the Chesil Bank, a deep ditch bounds the fields and then there is a scrubby hedge on the seaward side of the ditch. Extreme storm waves and human trampling along the coast path on the gravel beach control the seaward extent of the scrub. Here the hedge is almost entirely composed of blackthorn, which rarely produces fruit, and a few patches of bramble. The bushes vary from about 2m in height on the landward side, to virtually nil on the beach side. In one of the hedges, which is more or less isolated from any other hedges further inland,

An overgrown hedgerow. Not so many dormouse nests have been found here, as in some of the lower scrub nearer the sea. This is because in such mature bushes there are fewer structures in which a dormouse could anchor its nest

> so long as the **hedges** are at least a metre or two wide after cutting, **dormice** are most probably present

The Common Dormouse 39

not only had dormice nested on the landward side but also a mere metre from the seaward edge of the hedge. The nest was some 50cm off the ground in scrub only 80cm high. In another area behind the Chesil Bank, I have found nests in low scrub patches just above the beach, which are separated from any other scrub by a track way.

Although dormice doubtless might prefer large unmanaged hedgerows, I have found enough evidence from nests in managed hedges inland to consider that, so long as the hedges are at least a metre or two wide after cutting, dormice are most probably present. Such hedges are usually tightly flailed each year and produce few flowers or fruit. There are unfortunately many "hedges" in the areas of arable farming that are so viciously slashed each year one could not expect any self-respecting dormouse to consider them as arboreal habitat. In these areas the unsuitability of the hedges is compounded by the spray drift from the fields, which further depletes any food supplies. I have yet to explore the limits of dormouse tolerance to modern mechanised hedgerow management, but dormice have been found nesting in a tightly flailed hedge only 1.5m in height and 1m wide.[1]

In most counties along the south coast and in the Welsh borderlands there generally remains a good network of thick hedges, despite their being trimmed each year. In these areas the hedgerows were mainly constructed when the last remnants of the ancient woodlands were being cleared, and many of them may have at least a thousand years of continuity.[2] Dormice are

above: Hedge abutting the Chesil Bank. A dormouse nest was found in the bramble in the foreground, only a meter in from the path

below: One of the regularly trimmed hedges in which dormouse nests have been found. They are similarly found in hedges where there are no trees

probably widespread in all such areas. Devon is particularly well endowed with some 40,000km of hedgerows, which, combined, form a larger area of habitat than deciduous woodland in the county. It is not surprising that dormice have now been found to be widespread across Devon. In areas such as the Midlands, where the woods were mostly cleared for open pastures and the hedges were not planted until the Enclosure Acts in the eighteenth and nineteenth centuries, dormice may be much rarer in the hedges. But they survived in these regions where woods remained and doubtless have had enough time to spread out into the hedges, but no one appears to have looked for them.

Dormice in buildings

Dormice frequently enter buildings, which is hardly surprising as they are so often reported living in gardens. There are even reports of them entering buildings on a regular basis.[1] The most bizarre report I have heard was of a little old lady who lived in a wooden cottage in a wood in west Dorset. Dormice regularly entered her house and one lived in her piano! Most other reports are of more accidental visits, such as the one found curled up inside a make-up bag upstairs in a house in Shropshire.[2] A friend who lived on the north Devon coast knew one had got into his house, but could not find it. It was finally found the next day curled up asleep in a bowl of peaches: not a bad attempt at camouflage! Dormice have also on occasion been found feeding in buildings, anything from bread in a house, to sheep feed in a shed. And they often hibernate in out-houses and among the bales in hay barns. I know of three such cases locally.

> dormice have also on occasion been found **feeding** in buildings, anything from **bread** in a house to sheep feed in a barn

Dormouse tolerance of human disturbance

It is said that dormice are secretive animals, unable to tolerate human disturbance. This does not seem to be the case, judging by the nests I have found: one only a metre from a stile on a footpath, and many very near roads, as close as 30cm to the tarmac. Recent work carried out for the Highways Agency has found dormice living in numerous sites along some of the busiest main roads in Dorset. There are reports from other areas that they live so close to major roads that the trees are swayed by passing lorries.[1]

In the wild part of our garden, many nests are very close to pathways that are used regularly. There are more and more reports of dormice using bird feeders in gardens, even during daylight hours.

Dormouse nest built in the scrub by the road into West Bexington Village: only 30cm in from the edge of the tarmac

The Common Dormouse

Movement and dispersal of dormice

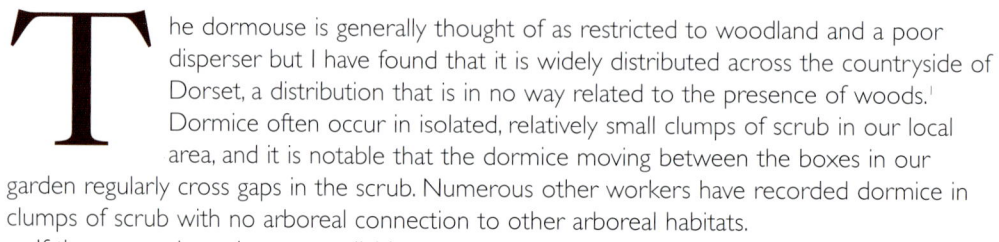

The dormouse is generally thought of as restricted to woodland and a poor disperser but I have found that it is widely distributed across the countryside of Dorset, a distribution that is in no way related to the presence of woods.[1] Dormice often occur in isolated, relatively small clumps of scrub in our local area, and it is notable that the dormice moving between the boxes in our garden regularly cross gaps in the scrub. Numerous other workers have recorded dormice in clumps of scrub with no arboreal connection to other arboreal habitats.

If there are arboreal routes available, there is no need for dormice to descend to ground level, and they are more nimble on branches than on the ground, as I have witnessed with escapees from boxes. However, they readily come to ground level to collect nesting material and for food. They are not confined to particular habitats and appear perfectly able to disperse and move across open ground when necessary. To have reached some of the patches of scrub where I have found their nests, dormice must have crossed track ways, and I have been told of several occasions when they have been seen crossing roads. There is even a record of them inhabiting a broadleaf plantation in the central reservation between the dual carriageways of the A303 in Cornwall.[2] In Germany a marked dormouse was reported to have migrated 450m between separate woods, and at least 250m of this was over open fields.[3] Few studies of dormice have been carried out over large enough areas to know how far young dormice travel when dispersing, but some have been reported to cover relatively long distances within woodland. A movement of 1,000m has been recorded in a Dorset wood, and in Continental forests there are records of 1,200m and up to 3,300m.

The road into West Bexington. Dormice nest in the isolated scrub patch on the right hand side of the road

Living with Dormice

Conservation management for dormice

A good thick hedge with a conservation strip of wildflowers to attract insects is just what helps all wildlife – not just dormice

The dormouse is widespread, at least in the south of England, but very elusive. It can probably be held to be a universal denizen in most arboreal habitats in areas where a network of hedgerows remain. It can thrive in nearly all types of woodland, from ancient broad-leaved woodland to modern conifer plantation and does well in most types of arboreal habitat, from patches of low growing scrub to woodland with a closed canopy of mature trees. In most woods it is doubtful that any specific management would be of help to it.

The advent of modern intensive farming has degraded and destroyed much wildlife habitat, and is probably a major cause of any decline in dormouse distribution and abundance. In most areas thickets and scrub have been removed from farmland, many hedges have been uprooted, and those remaining are closely cut each year. Modern hedgerow management, which involves cutting hedges every year with tractor-mounted flails, impoverishes them for wildlife. However, dormice will use hedges that are flailed each year. Flailing of hedgerows unfortunately often occurs soon after harvest time, which can be the peak breeding time for dormice. Even roadside hedges are now cut earlier and earlier, well before the dormice have finished breeding. A change in timing to winter would be of great benefit, as they would hopefully be less disturbed when in hibernation. This would then give dormice similar protection to that given to nesting birds. With

The Common Dormouse   43

the present change in emphasis from over-production to promoting environmental enhancement, it is hoped that hedgerow management will in future be more wildlife friendly.

Scrub is a valuable habitat in its own right, not just for dormice but also for a wide range of species, and the interface between scrub and grassland is an important habitat for a range of species. Scrub should be kept back from invading ecologically valuable grassland, but where it has already shaded out all herbs, it should perhaps be kept for its own sake as scrub brings nutrients to the surface layers and removal may result in weedy patches. So often management of scrub in grassland consists of the removal of whole patches of scrub, when surely keeping the invading edges back over the whole area would be more beneficial.

Management of woods and hedgerows has always been carried out in the countryside and does not appear to have generally harmed dormice. However, now that such management is usually mechanised, there may be more dire repercussions to their welfare if large areas are cut at the same time. Any management is likely to displace dormice and can have unfortunate results, as dormice appear to be very territorial. Only small areas should be managed each year, and preferably in winter when dormice are in hibernation.

Licences are officially needed for operations in habitat in which dormice are known to be nesting, even where planning permission is not required. In many areas dormice appear to be so widespread that any management of the countryside, even tree felling or hedge laying could result in unlawful disturbance and fatalities. But it would be ridiculous to say that such practices should not be carried out. Dormice are being found to be so widespread in every type of arboreal habitat, including rhododendron – a bane to almost all habitats – that any land managers could be so overwhelmed by paperwork and red tape that no work would ever get done. Nests are likely to be noticed only by observant workers, who could be penalised for their observance.

No studies appear to have been carried out to ascertain the fate of displaced animals. I have only circumstantial evidence of the results of displacement. Because of the timing for completing work for grants, one of the hedgerows in which I had boxes was laid in late October, before I had carried out the October box check. I was not surprised to find only five dormice in over sixty boxes on the whole site, as the check was carried out rather later than usual. It was notable that two of the five dormice were in boxes just beyond either end of the cut part of the hedge. In one was a female with most of her tail very freshly bitten off, and in the other a male of just under 15 grams. When I checked the boxes again two weeks later, the male had not put on any more weight, and a month after he had first been seen he was found dead. It seems therefore that dormice, like most small mammals are highly territorial, so that any displacement of them can have dire consequences.

There is as yet no reliable method of determining the real population density of dormice; therefore we cannot tell which is the "best" habitat for them. It would be expedient to know such a habitat if the dormouse is as rare as currently supposed, but in reality it appears to be widespread and in good numbers over a large area of Britain. It does well in thick hedges, patches of scrub and woodland of any size and almost any composition of species. If such habitats are preserved then the dormouse should be provided for adequately. Conservation of habitats for single species, in the present state of ecological knowledge, can have disastrous consequences, and it seems more prudent to aim at leaving a mosaic of habitats. The more extreme "restoration" policies, that seem to be today's fashion, are rather too drastic on the basis of present-day knowledge of ecological factors. It would be advisable for a more considered approach to be taken, and if there are any doubts, for habitat to be left alone.

Some of you will be wondering why I have not mentioned such activities as coppicing hazel for dormice: it is covered in a later section.

left: An example of a hedgerow that is almost flailed out of existence every year

below: It is a great pity that so many hedgerows are so savagely flailed each year. Occasionally overgrown hedgerows can be found along old trackways, or in this case along a stream in the valley of Loscombe, West Dorset

The Common Dormouse 45

Dormouse nests

Dormice build two main types of nest: ones they use in summer when they are active and ones in winter in which they hibernate.

The nests are roughly spherical in shape and are woven from a fibrous material, which is usually grass. They have no definite entrance hole. Summer nests can be found anywhere from ground level to high up in the tops of trees, but hibernation is usually near ground level in a more tightly woven nest. There are few other nests that can be confused with dormouse nests. Domed birds' nests, such as those of the wren, have a distinct entrance hole and usually contain a lot of moss in their construction. The nests of harvest mice (*Micromys minutus*) are probably most similar to those of dormice, but are generally of a tidier appearance and are usually made only of grass. A useful diagnostic character of harvest mouse nests is that the mice have a habit of finely splitting the grass leaves longitudinally. Harvest mouse nests are usually anchored among coarse grasses but can be found in the edges of grassy scrub, and I have at times found them higher in the scrub than nearby dormouse nests.

opposite: Dormouse summer nest with a woven grass interior and well 'thatched' with leaves from various trees

Hibernation Nests

Dormouse hibernation nests are about the size of a tennis ball and are more tightly woven than summer nests, with no suggestion of an entrance, so that the animal seems completely sealed up inside. They are usually so tightly woven that they are virtually waterproof. I know of one that was found floating down a flooded track-way with the occupant still dry inside. Often the way that such nests are identified is by the occupant, but they can be so well constructed that considerable unpicking may be required before any animal is visible! They are primarily woven from grass but any other local material can be incorporated in them. The hibernation nests are usually found at or near ground level, where the temperature is relatively constant and where there is enough moisture to prevent the animals becoming dehydrated.

Hibernation nests can be found on the ground, barely covered by moss or fallen leaves, but are usually well hidden where they are unlikely to be discovered. Lengthy hunting can find them in more accessible sites such as hazel coppices, and woodmen were said to have been able to locate them in the spring by putting their ear to woodland banks and hearing the wheezing noise that dormice make when waking up. They are also commonly found low down in the stool of a tree or shrub, and in coarse tussocks of grasses and sedges. Dormice also hide their hibernation nests under log piles, or rocks, or

Three hibernation nests found among the rocks on a rockery. The dormice are still asleep inside them

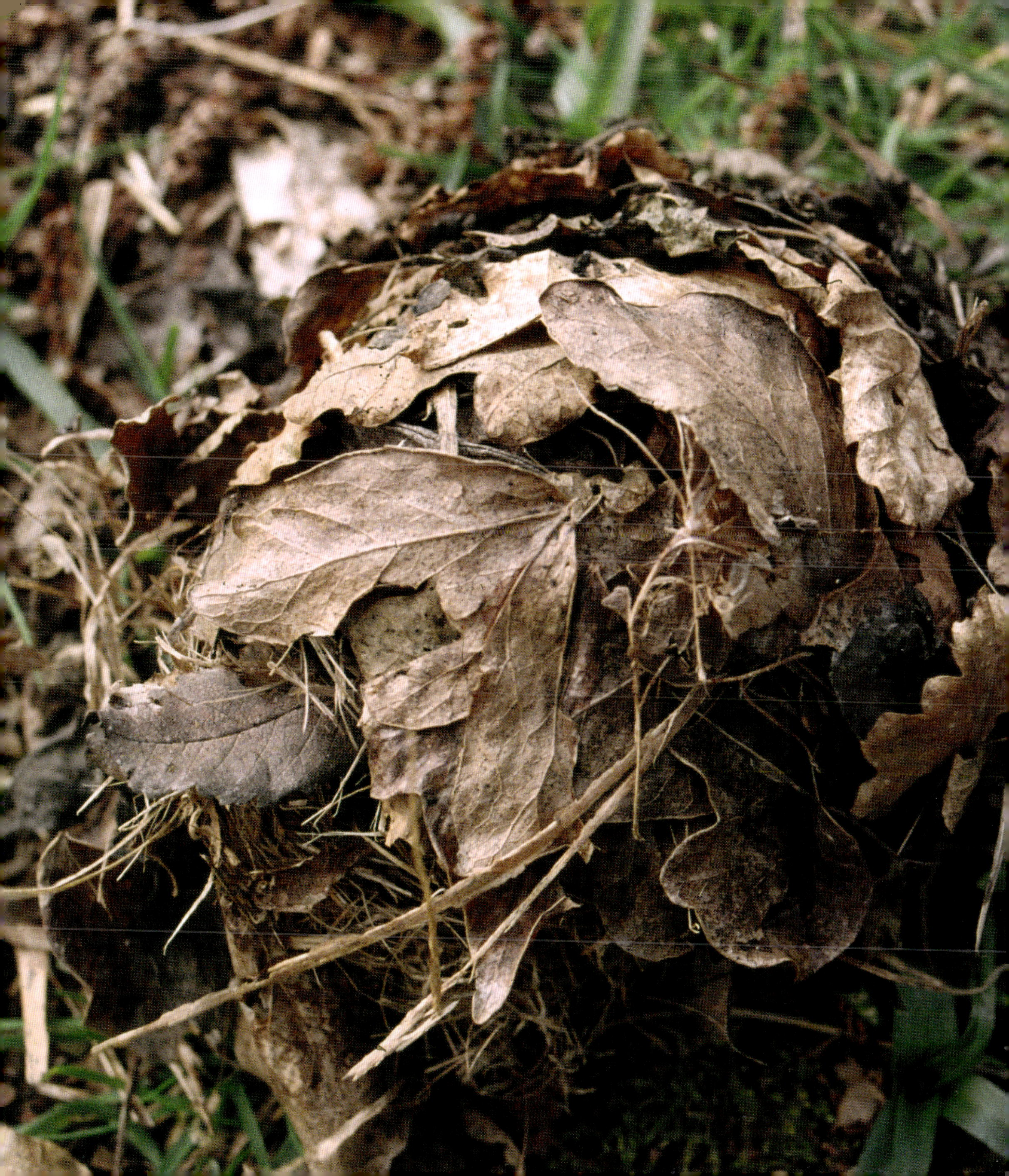

above: Dormouse nest from a box where much of the material is bracken

top: Summer nest out of a nest box, showing the most usual construction. The outer layer consists of green leaves with an inner nest of woven grass. The moss is from the start of a tit's nest

even among bales in hay barns. Nests have been reported from below ground level, but such discoveries are for obvious reasons rather rare. Generally, hibernation nests are most likely to be located by accident, and I know of several occasions where this has happened in local gardens. A neighbour was tidying up a clump of pampas grass when a nest rolled out; another friend was digging up a shrub and found more than just roots. On a further occasion a rockery was being revamped and three nests were found among the rocks. The strangest find I have been shown was a hibernation nest buried in the top of a plant pot containing a shrub, and that was the second year that a dormouse had hibernated in the same pot! The more bizarre records of hibernation sites include a woollen hat in a garden shed, inside a child's foam filled ball in an outhouse, and even under the blanket on the back seat of a car. But then there are reports of them nesting in old mattresses in back gardens, but I have not been given permission to test this yet![1]

Summer Nests

Dormouse summer nests are of somewhat looser construction than their hibernation nests. They are about 8-15cm in diameter, the larger ones being breeding nests. Dormice build and use several nests within their home range at any given time, which led the Victorians to mistakenly assume that the dormouse was rather gregarious in its habits, rather than territorial.[2] The summer nests are made in a diagnostic form with woven fibrous material and some broad leaves incorporated in the outer layer, but dormice are far too resourceful in using whatever material is at hand for the actual material used to be diagnostic. It is usually stated that the main fibrous material in their construction is honeysuckle bark. Honeysuckle is common in the habitats where they are usually studied. Where honeysuckle is present it is rational that dormice use it, as it saves them a journey down to ground level to collect grass. Stripping of honeysuckle bark may indicate the presence of dormice, but they are not the only creatures to do this. Dormice live in many habitats devoid of honeysuckle and here grass is the predominant material used. In nest boxes I have known them to replace grass with leaves of bracken or other fern, the stems of recently mown soft rush, or dead bluebell leaves.

The leaves on the outside are usually collected as near the nest as possible, so are usually ones growing on nearby branches. The colour of the leaves is sometimes given as a guide to identifying a dormouse nest rather than a wood mouse nest. Wood mice usually use brown leaves collected from the ground. When dormice collect green leaves off the branches, especially in the case of hazel, the leaves tend to dry to a greyish colour rather than brown. This can be diagnostic, but dormice often collect dead leaves from ground level, especially early in the season. In nest boxes they can almost fill the space with leaves before weaving a nest of fibrous material in the centre. At one site where the leaves in the nest boxes were counted, several had over a hundred and in one case over five hundred had been used.[3]

Dormice often site their nests not far from a source of suitable nesting material, but this is not always the case. They have been reported nesting in a junction box at the top of a telephone pole, which did not abut any trees.[4] So perhaps the suitability and security of the site are more important than the proximity of materials. Dormice use a wide range of nesting materials, and it is surprising what they will use when nest building. Where the nests are positioned in bushes with rather small leaves, such as blackthorn, the dormice go down to ground level to find larger leaves. I have seen the leaves of hart's tongue fern used on several occasions. Prickles certainly do not deter them: they use anything from bramble leaves to thistle leaves. Perhaps most surprisingly, on several occasions I have found that they had used stinging nettle leaves (I do not know how they pick or carry them, presumably carefully!). The outer leaves of the nest usually look as if they are added to act as a thatch, so perhaps it is a shame that dormice do not realise that nettle leaves shrink when dry, and would therefore seem to be fairly useless for nest construction.

above: Dormouse summer nest woven from honeysuckle bark. Honeysuckle has been said to be almost essential for nest building. But dormice are adaptive creatures and just use what is available

left: Summer nest in the scrub in our garden

far left: A dormouse Summer nest built of grass and leaves among bramble

The Common Dormouse

Hibernation

When an animal is in torpor it is inactive and there is a reduction of its body temperature. Torpor is generally thought to be driven by ambient temperature and food availability. Hibernation is an extended form of torpor, thought to be associated with day length and hormonal changes. Dormice are one of the few British mammals, apart from bats, which truly hibernate; but in other parts of the world many small mammals use hibernation to escape from cold temperatures and consequent scarcity of food. By suppressing their metabolic rate and allowing their body temperature to fall near the ambient temperature, species such as the dormouse can survive for six months or more living off body fat reserves. The core body temperature of the animals is still controlled so that it is greater than the ambient temperature, and so prevents the animals from freezing.

Seasonal hibernation is a poorly understood phenomenon and details of how hibernation induction, maintenance and arousal are controlled are for the most part enigmatic. Morphological data suggests that hibernation is not merely a condition of reduced activity and metabolism, but involves active rearrangement of several cell and tissue constituents. Total energy savings in such animals are not absolute as all hibernators go through periodic rapid arousals during their hibernation season, when they return briefly to normal active body temperatures. The functions of the arousals remain a mystery, although they must serve some essential function. The usual hypothesis for this intermittent warming is that it eliminates some chemical imbalance that accumulates during periods of low body temperature. Another feasible explanation is that a normal active body temperature may be essential to maintain lymphocyte numbers and hence maintain the animal's immunity, as many pathogens remain virulent at cold temperatures. I find dormice bites rarely leave any soreness at all. Is it that their saliva contains some sort of antibacterial agent, a feature that would be advantageous to a hibernator whose immune system might not be functioning normally at low temperatures? Dormice are held to be a particularly ancient group of rodents and it is thought that their ability to go so readily into torpor may be a primitive characteristic.

When hibernating the body of a dormouse feels cold to the touch, and it is rolled up into a ball, with its tail wrapped up over its nose. This small compact ball of fur has been described as "a delightful thing to see and hold."[1] The length of hibernation varies in different regions of the Continent. In southern areas it is short and shallow. In Sicily dormice can be active and breed in winter, whereas in northern latitudes they may hibernate for six or even seven months. In Britain they usually go into hibernation by the time of the first frosts, some time in October or November, and come out in April or May. Timings vary with the weather, and some dormice down by the coast in Dorset are usually using boxes a month earlier and go into hibernation a month later than those only a

An adult hibernating dormouse found among pampas grass in a neighbour's garden. When found at the beginning of April he was 23 grams, still well above summer weight

Living with Dormice

A hibernating dormouse curled up in a very tight ball

few miles inland. Arousal as early as March was a fairly widespread event after the warm winter of 2006-7. The earliest arousals appear to be underweight juveniles, perhaps those from an extra late brood.

Only very rarely are dormice found using nest boxes during the winter months. They usually build their hibernation nests near ground level, where the temperature and moisture levels are more constant. On the Continent dormice have been recorded leaving the nest and foraging during wintertime, but there appear to be no such reports from Britain. On a couple of occasions I have had dormice move in or out of boxes during the early and late months of hibernation, when they appeared to be in hibernation mode. Earlier writings suggest that they may collect winter stores of food,[2] but no recent reports confirm this, and such a tactic could be dangerous, as the food would attract other rodents. While in hibernation the dormouse is very vulnerable to disturbance and predation.

In captivity dormice have been found to put on weight rapidly just before hibernation.[3] By more frequent monitoring of the dormice in coastal sites in the autumn, I have found that dormice in the wild also have a very rapid weight gain just before hibernation. This must surely be because they do not want to carry excess weight any longer than absolutely necessary, as it

The Common Dormouse

Hibernation nest found in the pampas grass in a neighbour's garden

by suppressing their metabolic rate dormice can survive for six months or more living off body fat reserves

would make them more vulnerable to predators. The most rapid weight gain that I have recorded was in one young dormouse that doubled its weight from 14 grams to 28 grams in only ten days. Once a dormouse starts to pile on weight, most succeed in achieving the necessary weight gain in two weeks. From my observations it appears that young dormice need to grow to about 15 grams before they are adult enough for the rapid weight gain needed for hibernation.[4] I have found young dormice of about 15 grams still active in boxes even in December after snow (a rare occurrence by the coast). If 15 grams was heavy enough for hibernation, they would surely not have been active in such cold weather.

From the several occasions that I have been able to recapture dormice in nest boxes during the autumn, it appears that they generally reach about 28 grams before disappearing to hibernate. This weight is in good agreement with the hibernation weights found in young dormice in studies on the Continent.[5] Higher weights are found, mainly among adult dormice; the heaviest I have recorded was 43.5 grams in one male.

Waifs and injured dormice that I have brought in during November and December usually put on weight very rapidly, and although they do not always achieve 28 grams they have always reached well over 20 grams before showing any inclination to go into torpor. On 23rd December one year I was brought a dormouse that had been mauled by a cat. It weighed only 16 grams, but even though it was too ill to eat for a couple of days, and had to have antibiotic injections for several days, it was 21 grams by the New Year.

Dormice readily eat insects as well as nuts and fruit, and in many habitats it may be insects that form the main food supply needed before hibernation. However, it is still something of a

52 *Living with Dormice*

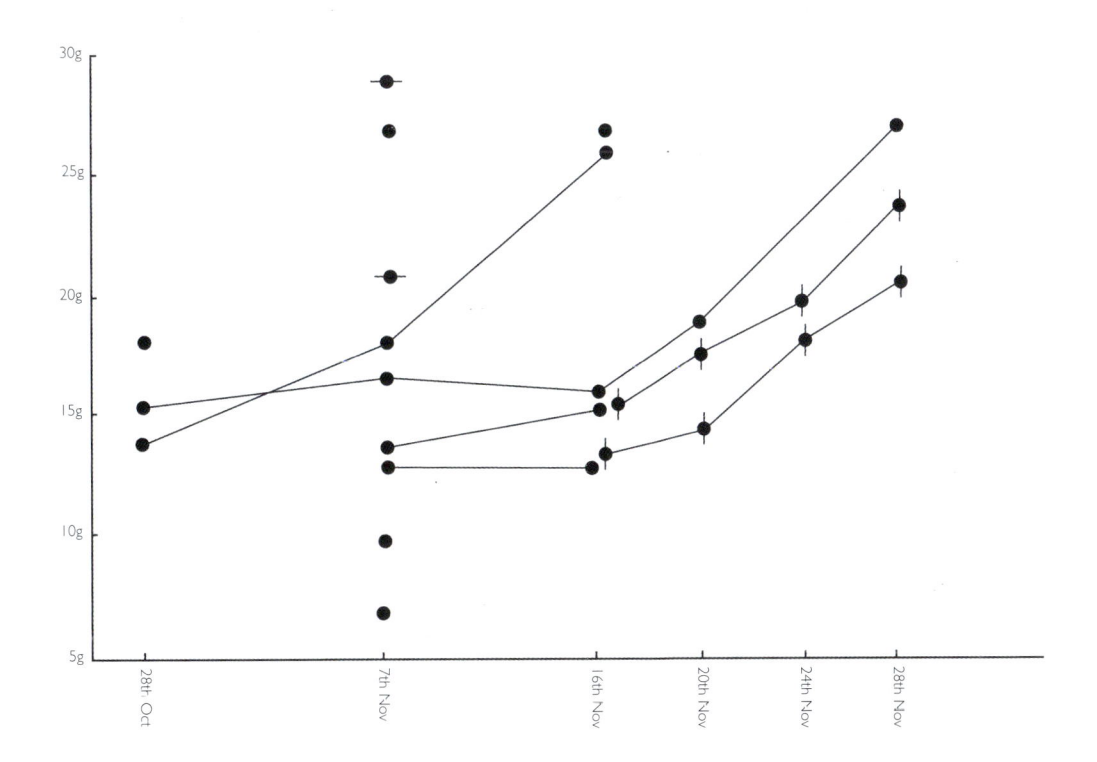

mystery as to what they can find to eat in blackthorn scrub in late November or even December in some years, that still enables them to rapidly increase their weight before hibernation, a good month after the leaves and fruits have been stripped off the bushes by the autumn gales.

The dormice seem to have coped well with the succession of very mild winters we have had on the Dorset coast, and in April some hibernators have been found to weigh as much as 23 grams, well over their normal summer weight; but this weight soon decreases. Their weight on first arousal cannot be judged from those in nest boxes, as they may have been active for sometime before using the boxes and the low weights often found in dormice in boxes in the spring would seem to be due to the dormice, especially the males, having other priorities than feeding!

above: Unpicking the nest does indeed reveal a furry body

top: The weights of four of the juvenile dormice found in the nest boxes at West Bexington Reserve in the late autumn of 2002. They show how rapidly dormice can put on the extra weight that they need in preparation for hibernation. Different symbols denote dormice found in different boxes

The Common Dormouse

54   Living with Dormice

Summer torpor

In addition to hibernating, dormice can go into torpor for part of the day during their active part of the year. They feel cold to the touch and can take up to twenty minutes to fully wake up. They may forage during the early part of the night and then enter torpor for eight or more hours, arousing from torpor as their surroundings warm up during the morning.

Torpor is little understood and is generally considered as an adaptation to save energy at times of difficulty, such as during periods of inclement weather or seasonal food shortage. However, it has been shown to occur in some species where there is no shortage of food, and it is suggested that it may be more a strategy, not just to save energy, but may be useful to retain or build up energy stores. This idea tallies with the tale of a pet dormouse, which was found in torpor after a night when it had eaten 149 fine hawk-moth caterpillars.[1] Torpor occurs mostly in the early or late parts of the active season of dormice. It may be less common in midsummer because the opportunities for gaining energetic advantage are reduced when it is not cold enough.

I have found that on some sites when dormice are checked in the mornings, up to 50 per cent of the animals may be in torpor in the early part of their active season. In the summer months I have only found dormice, and only males, in torpor when the weather is exceptionally cold and wet. In the autumn the only time I find them in torpor is when they have put on weight and are just about ready to go into hibernation.

above: In the spring groups of young adult dormice are often found together

left: If woken from torpor dormice try to hide from the sun

opposite: A dormouse in torpor with its tail over its nose is not easily forgotten!

The Common Dormouse

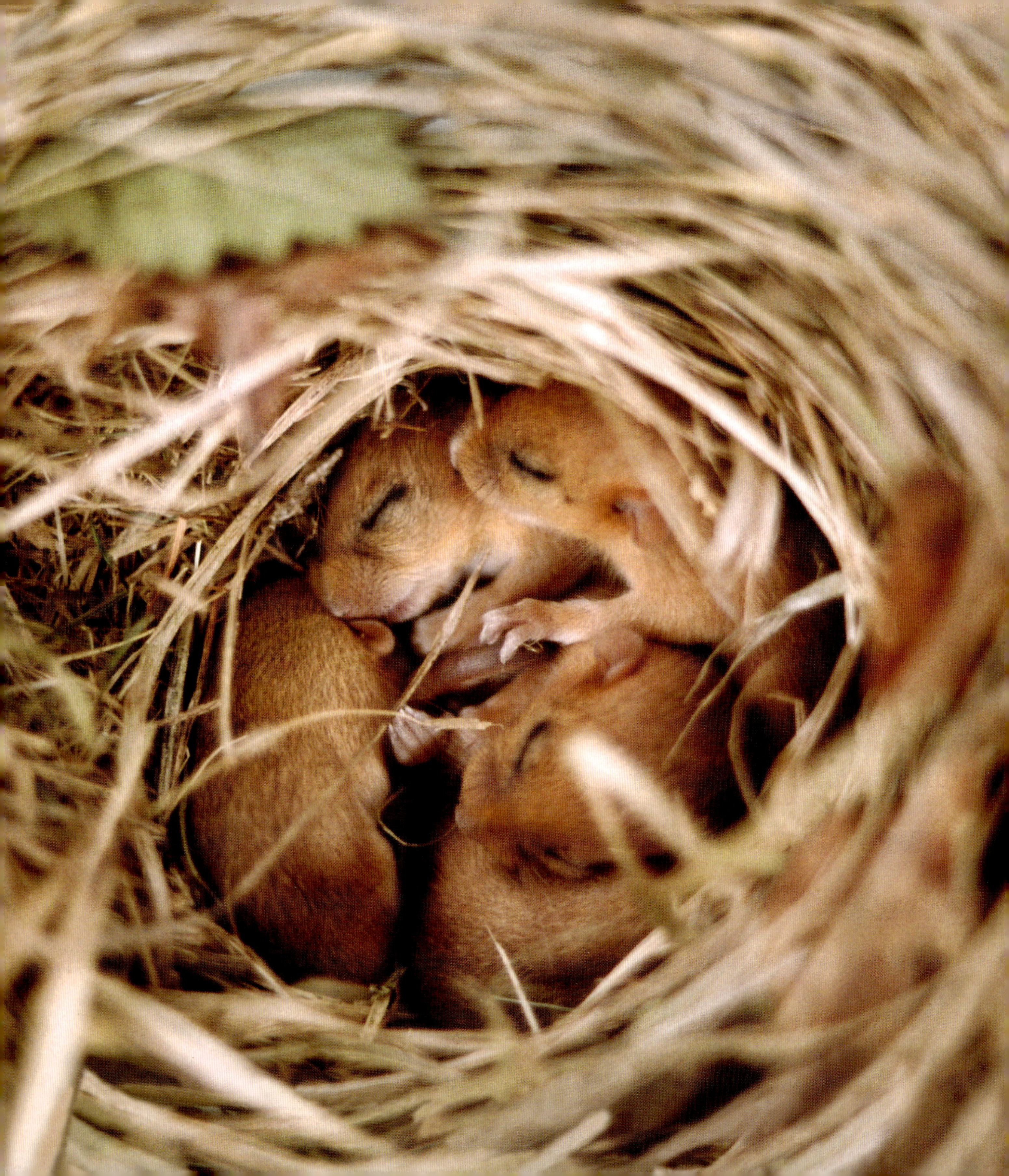

Breeding in dormice

The breeding strategy of dormice is different from that of most small rodents. The life span of most mice, such as wood mice, in the wild is usually measured in months, and they can produce up to five or six large broods of young each year. Dormice, on the other hand, produce relatively few young each year, but can have a much longer life span of up to five years in the wild. Breeding nests of dormice are larger and more substantial than the ordinary summer nests and are lined with soft material. This can be just chewed up grass, but also such material as the fine hairs from willow seeds, willowherb seeds or thistle down, and even sheep's wool caught on nearby brambles or barbed wire.

The brood cycle in dormice takes about two months. The gestation period is just over twenty days. Young dormice are born naked and blind, their eyes open after about a fortnight. Their mothers feed them for about four weeks before they venture from the nest. It is a further couple of weeks or more before the young become independent, during which time they are thought to go out with their mother on foraging trips. Dormice tolerate humans handling their young, even when only days old. This is presumably to do with the greater investment that they appear to put into their young, compared with faster breeding rodents, such as wood mice. Young dormice may be as much as 12 grams when they are first independent of their mothers, but in autumn I have found some deserted by their mothers as small as 7 grams. It seems that after the first frosts the urge of the adults to hibernate may be greater than their maternal instincts.

In captivity dormice are able to produce two or three broods a year. Similarly, in some places on the Continent it is suggested that dormice have at least two or three broods a year, and there seems no reason why this should not apply in Britain as well. Many sites, including some of my own and also sites on the much colder north slopes of Dartmoor, have recorded young being born in May. Even with each brood taking about two months to rear, it still means that it is possible for three broods to be reared in a year. I have on several occasions recorded two broods from the same mother, but my only proof of three broods in one season is somewhat circumstantial. In tubes in one hedgerow I first found a brood of young, heavy enough to be independent of a mother, the following month I found a mother with small young, and she subsequently had a further brood that year.

Dormice are rodents and therefore should be expected to breed throughout their active season. In Lithuania, where dormice have been studied in forests further north than the range of wood mice, the breeding season occupies nearly the whole of their shorter summer season. Here animals are found in breeding condition even in late April, when there may still be snow on the ground. And many females appear to have two broods with a peak in births in May/June and another in August. The mean size of the litters was found to depend on the age of the

above: Breeding nest. These are bigger and better constructed than most summer nests. The inner lining is made of finely shredded material. Some of the eight young are just visible along with the mother's tail

opposite: Here the young are well furred but their eyes are still closed

The Common Dormouse

above: Dormice are born naked with their eyes closed. These are several days old and just beginning to get some grey fur

above: Almost two weeks on their eyes are still closed, but they are quick to try and scrabble away from danger

mothers. It was the younger dormice, probably born in the second broods of the previous year, which appeared to breed only once, in July or August, but often dormice born early in the year bred in the same year as they were born.[2] In comparison, three broods a year for older dormice would seem quite reasonable in the longer summers of Britain. Families of young are often found in Britain in September or even later.

Nest boxes are anything but a satisfactory means of observing the true breeding potential of dormice. Boxes are usually used only by younger dormice in their first breeding season, and they start breeding later and have smaller broods. The second broods of dormice, after they have put on more weight, are usually larger. Earlier breeders are probably more mature animals, and will have larger broods of young. It seems that these more experienced mothers generally avoid using boxes and the dangers associated with them.

The brood size of dormice is usually given as four or five but the majority of the broods that I have recorded have been five or more, and twice I have recorded as many as nine young. Such large numbers have at times been interpreted as females aggregating their families into a crèche. I have never seen evidence of this. Breeding of dormice born in the same year has been recorded on the Continent and found to occur frequently in Lithuania. In Britain dormice are said not to breed until after their first winter, but I have recorded females on three occasions with well-grown youngsters, and have on several occasions found males to be sexually active, in the same year as they were born.

It would appear that the breeding potential of the dormouse has been underestimated, as well as possible predation levels. As in most animal populations, it is probable that the turnover is far more dynamic with few individuals reaching a ripe old age and most young succumbing to predators in their first year, although with the relatively low breeding potential of dormice, population changes are unlikely to be comparable to the massive fluctuations that occur in the populations of the shorter-lived, more fecund voles and mice.

Living with Dormice

Predation of dormice

Dormice are very elusive and rarely seen. Signs of their presence need to be carefully hunted for, so evidence of predation is even more unlikely to be found. Also, they live in much smaller numbers than most of the rodents that are the common prey of predators and so will be taken in much smaller numbers. But dormice are just small rodents, food for anything that can get them, and most mouse-eating predators can fly or climb trees. So it would hardly seem feasible, as has been suggested, that dormice have few predators and that if they keep in the branches away from the ground they are relatively safe and rarely preyed on. If disturbed, dormice freeze up in the branches and may stay immobile for anything up to three quarters of an hour before moving again. This must be a device to escape detection by predators.

Owls are likely to be one of the most deadly of predators, and their food, by means of their pellets, can be easily studied. On the Continent dormice are regularly taken by owls, although they rarely comprise more than 10 per cent of all prey items. In Britain less than one per cent of owl pellets are said to contain dormouse remains and therefore it has been concluded that owls are not a real threat to dormice. Even at this level it shows that owls do take dormice, and in view of the relative scarcity of dormice in comparison with other rodents this could still be significant. The tawny owl is a woodland owl and therefore the most likely to take them. At least locally, it could be a significant predator, especially in years when populations of other small rodents have crashed. At one of the inland sites where I have boxes, pellet analysis showed that a tawny owl had taken several dormice in three successive years, and in one year they constituted 8 per cent of its prey in the pellet samples. However, the latter result could have been an indication of the danger of nest boxes to dormice, as the tawny owl had its roost in a tree next to one on which a nest box was fixed and in which dormice bred: the owl had removed the equivalent of the entire brood. At the same site dormouse remains were found in the pellets of barn owls. Little owls are chiefly insect feeders, but have also been recorded feeding on dormice.

It is difficult to tell how much of a threat weasels are to dormice because of their secretive ways. They certainly kill and eat dormice in boxes, and dormice in torpor must constitute easy pickings for such a nimble climber. Reports of weasels raiding nest boxes are rare, but I have knowingly had it occur on two sites. It would seem that dormice can tolerate competition for food with grey squirrels, but when in torpor or with young, they must be in danger of being found by grey squirrels. It is

Owls are likely to be one of the most deadly of predators

Tawny owl: a woodland owl that feeds on dormice

Wood mouse at home in a dormouse box. Note the untidy nest of brown leaves

surprising that dormice so often make their nests in squirrels' dreys.

Dormice are probably at their most vulnerable when hibernating. As they arouse from hibernation their breathing is a rather noisy wheezing, which can be heard from some distance: it has even been described as like a small squeaky wheelbarrow. Such a noise could well attract predators. Dormice often hibernate on the ground, covered by just a thin layer of moss or leaves. Here they are vulnerable to floods, trampling and predation and probably exceedingly vulnerable to stoats, weasels, badgers and foxes. It has been reported that even magpies can locate them, and that a pheasant has been seen to find and eat one. Dormice are also at danger from other rodents, and to this long list of predators must now be added wild boar. The return of wild boar to British woods, although welcomed by some ecologists, is bad news for dormice, which are said to be particularly at risk from wild boar in Lithuania, especially when there is no snow on the ground.[1] I have very mixed feelings about the ecological advantages of wild boar, and personally would prefer to keep the dormice and bluebells! Britain at present has probably over 50 per cent of the world's bluebells, but for how much longer now wild boars are back? Pigs of any sort can spread foot-and-mouth disease, and exclusion of stock is advantageous to most woodland biota.

It is sometimes said that cats only infrequently catch dormice, but other reports in the literature state that cats are the most significant predators of dormice! It was held to be so important by some planners that they forbade occupants of a new housing estate to keep cats because dormice had been found in scrub adjacent to the site. It is doubtful that predation by cats is significant as they are not the nimblest of climbers. However, most cat owners to whom I have spoken in the West Dorset countryside admit that their cats do bring in dormice.

It's a mouse eat mouse world

Nest boxes are not safe homes for dormice. Here a dormouse has been feasted on by other mice

As well as actual predators there is the rival world. What rodent lives without constant rivalry, with not only its own sort but also with other rodents?

Wood mice may not generally be classed as predators, but they are voracious omnivores and have been reported eating the bodies of other wood mice. So what is a dormouse in torpor but a nice chunk of cold meat? Dormice are very vulnerable to attack when in torpor, and there are reports of wood mice eating out their brains.[1] Several dormice in the boxes on one of my sites have been attacked with similarly gruesome results. Wood mice must be considered very serious competitors of dormice, not only because they kill dormice when in torpor, but also because they regularly take over dormouse nests in both boxes and tubes. How often they take over dormouse nests anchored in branches is unknown, but from the position dormice often put their nests they must be significant competitors, and would certainly usurp dormouse nests in holes in trees. Yellow-necked mice are generally not as common as wood mice, but where present must similarly constitute a serious threat to dormice, especially if the way they attack fingers is anything to go by. They, too, take over

60 *Living with Dormice*

dormouse nests. These two species of mice are highly arboreal and must compete directly with dormice in much of their habitat.

Because most rodents can be trapped easily at ground level, there have been surprisingly few attempts to examine the use of the aerial parts of their arboreal habitats. Yellow-necked mice have been recorded up to a height of 23m in a tree and bank voles have been caught in traps up to 3m above ground level, so the dormouse is not alone up in the branches.[2] It has been suggested that the spatial activity of dormice compared with that of other rodents is likely to compensate for any overlap in diet between species. But the other species appear to be capable of being very arboreal and dormice often use scrub of only a metre in height. It remains an enigma how dormice manage to survive in habitats alongside more numerous rodents such as wood mice. Here they are not only in direct competition for food but also in danger of being killed by them. It is said that a good supply of fruits and nuts is essential to dormice before hibernation, but dormice can fatten up for hibernation in habitats where these are lacking. So it is salutary to think that a bad nut year could even help dormice, in that competitors in the form of wood and yellow-necked mice would have little in the way of winter stores and their numbers might possibly crash over the winter.

Rodents, other than mice, can be found using boxes, but this is far more infrequent. I have had only one box used by rats, which could be a significant threat to hibernating dormice. Bank voles are regularly found in boxes, but infrequently enough for them not to be a problem. There are years when I do not find any at all. But again they could be a threat to dormice in torpor as they have been recorded eating dead mice in traps. Some species of shrew have been reported eating dead mice, but the only species that regularly uses the boxes is the pygmy shrew, which is mainly an insectivore and does not seem to perturb dormice. On one occasion I even found a pygmy shrew in the same box as a dormouse; distracted by the shrew, the dormouse escaped!

As with many small animals, one of the chief dangers for dormice comes from their own kind. Many dormice are found with damaged tails, and sometimes, though rarely, no tail at all, when they look peculiarly like tree hamsters. Most dormice with damaged tails that I have seen have been males, which are territorial and aggressive in the breeding season. Damage to a tail can result in the hairs at the end being white, as I have witnessed in a dormouse that I recaptured one year, after first finding it with a raw wound at the end of its tail. In the Victorian era, when dormice were collected to be sold as pets, a white tip to the tail enhanced their market value!

above: The yellow-necked mouse is an aggressive rodent which is larger than the dormouse.

below left: Two dormice, both with damaged tails. It would seem that this is due to territorial fighting, rather than failed attacks by predators

below right: Damage to the tail of a dormouse can result in the subsequent growth of white hairs. About 10% of male dormice have lost a sizeable length of their tail through fighting, and many more have damage at least to the tips of their tails

The Common Dormouse

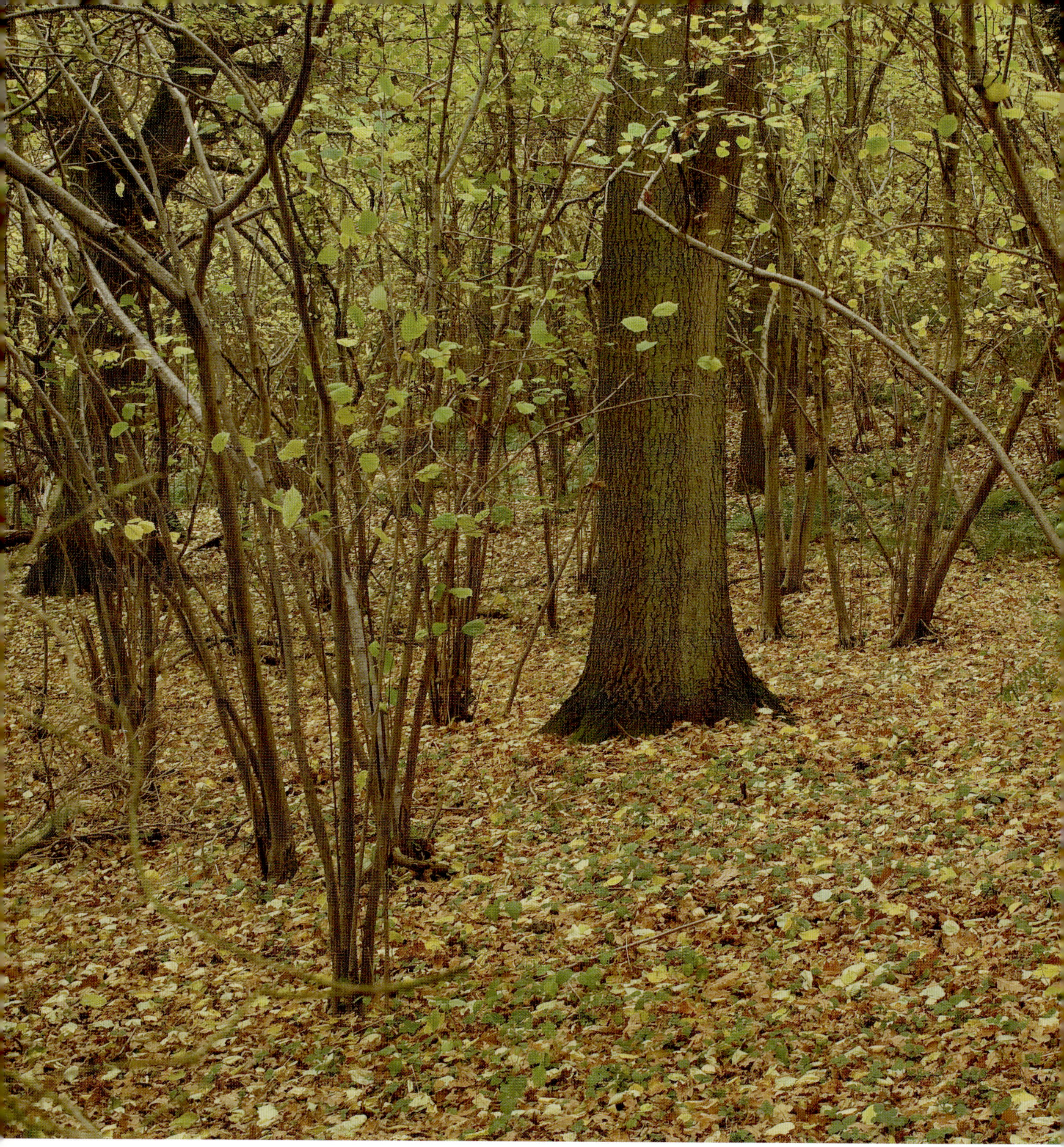

Surveying for dormice

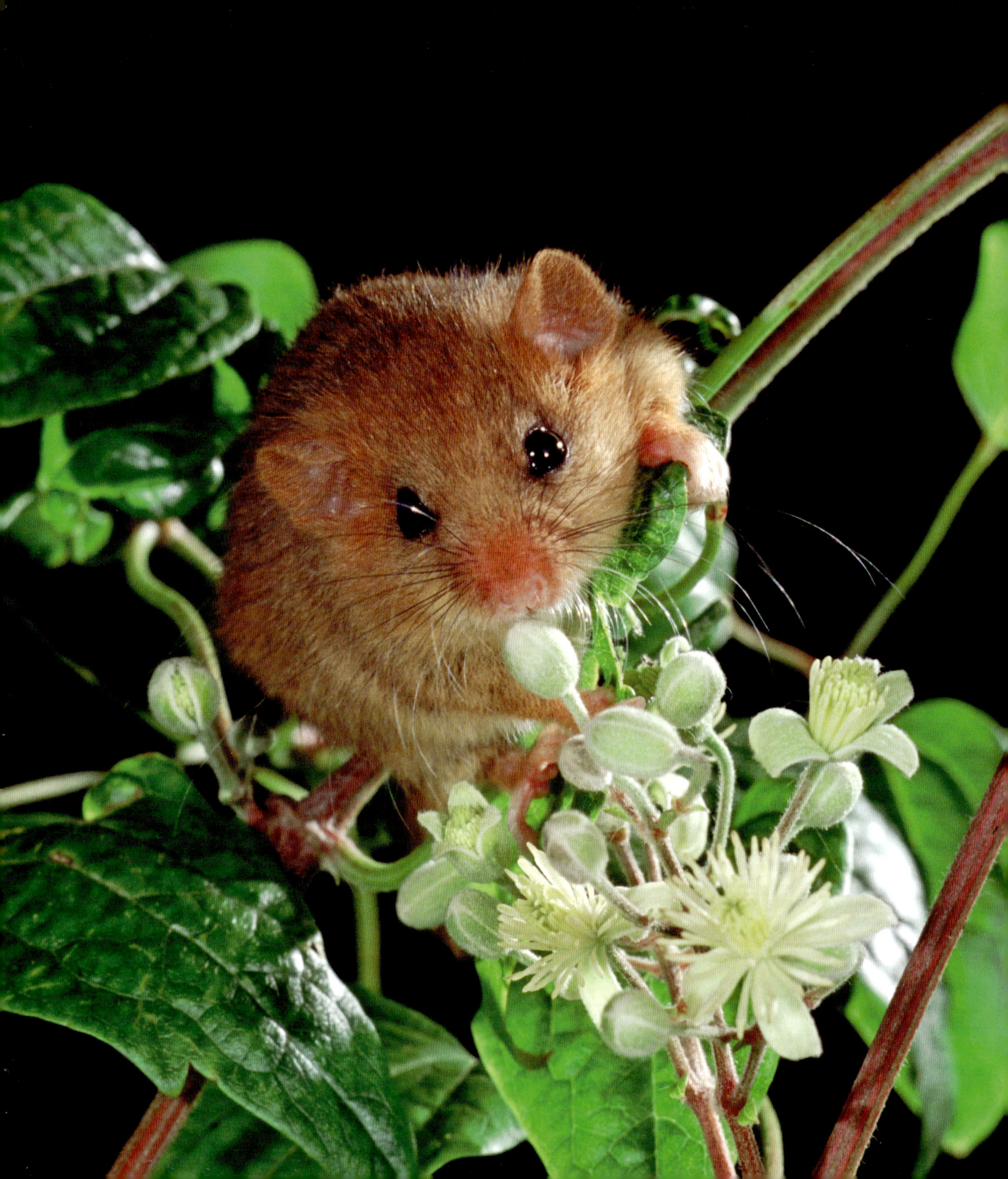

Dormice are almost impossible to see in the wild, even though guides to many nature reserves flaunt their presence, and intimate that they can be seen. It is unlikely that surveyors will meet with an actual dormouse unless they trap one or put up artificial nest sites, for which a licence is required. But the dormouse does leave definitive signs in the way it opens nuts and in the structure of its nest. This makes it easier to locate its haunts by just looking, than is the case for most other small mammals. But even looking for signs takes concentration, and they are not likely to be noticed unless one is specifically aware of such signs. If it had not been for an accident when clearing scrub, I doubt if we would ever have realised that there were dormice in our garden or in the surrounding hedges.

I have not tried all possible methods of surveying for dormice, such as trapping or using hair-tubes, where hairs are trapped on sticky tape and serve to identify the visiting animal. Both methods entail a lot of work with very low success rates. Although other small mammals climb trees and bushes, they spend enough time on the ground to be easily caught in traps, whereas dormice spend most of their time up in the branches and are rarely, if ever, caught in traps. It has been found that dormice can be caught using wire traps set up in branches, but catches are small. Recent trials in Wales showed that trapping is a feasible and relatively effective method of detecting dormouse presence, but is not easy as it is time consuming and the traps are most effective when attached to branches some 4-5m above ground level.[1]

I do not feel that the lifestyle of dormice is amenable to trapping. They hibernate for up to half the year, when they cannot be trapped and, except for a month or so at the beginning of the season, females with dependent young could be caught. Even a single night without their mother could cause the death of a brood of young dormice, so trapping hardly seems a responsible tactic when dealing with a supposedly rare animal that produces relatively few young each year.

No totally satisfactory method has as yet been found for surveying dormice, so failure to find them should never be taken as proof of absence. All methods are fraught with problems, which many surveyors have either brushed aside or not been aware of. Ignoring these problems has led to the belief that the dormouse is a rare animal. I have tried the most used methods of detecting dormouse presence – searching for eaten hazel nuts, searching for summer nests, and putting up artificial nesting sites. I first discuss in more detail the pros and cons of searches for nuts and nests. These are signs that anybody can look for in the countryside. Artificial nest sites need more commitment, as they have to be checked on a regular basis and to be kept in good condition. Once it has been established that dormice are present, a licence is required if they are to be disturbed. Before a licence can be obtained, some experience is needed. For this the best approach is to get in touch with your local Wildlife Trust or Mammal Group, if there is one in your area.

Dormice appear to live at lower densities than other small mammals, such as wood mice or bank voles. This may be because they are very territorial in the breeding season. The true densities at which they occur are not known but must be much higher than generally stated. There appears to be no universally workable method of detecting dormouse presence, let alone population densities. It would be difficult, if not impossible, to ever find the population size of dormice in any area using any of these methods. It can take many years just to prove that dormice are present, and many more years may be needed before any true idea of their abundance in any area can be ascertained.

previous page: Hazel coppice woodland. This habitat has previously been thought to be essential for dormice. But dormice are just as numerous in other habitats

opposite: Dormice are normally photographed in torpor, but this one is wide awake

Surveying for Dormice

Searching for hazel nuts eaten by <u>dormice</u>

Eaten hazel nuts are the most distinct and perhaps the most useful field signs for identifying the presence of dormice. Dormice open hazel nuts in a unique way, leaving a neat, round hole with smooth edges. Faint teeth marks run around the edge of the hole because the dormouse uses a scooping action when enlarging it. There are also teeth marks on the outside, on the nut surface, radiating out at an acute angle to the edge of the hole. The hole is usually on the side of the nut, incorporating part of the basal attachment zone of the nut. Wood mice make similar holes but leave distinct teeth marks at right angles across the edge of the hole (distinctive – but a hand lens helps). Wood mice also leave marks on the nut surface, but voles, which leave similar parallel grooves on the inner rim of the nut, do not leave teeth marks on the surface.

Some other hard fruits are opened in the same distinctive way by dormice. A friend, Jan Crowden, introduced me to some hawthorn pips opened by dormice, which she had been watching with a night scope. That same day we went to check some nest tubes and found sloe stones opened in an identical way. Searching for such evidence is feasible, but not easy hunting compared with hazel nuts. However, it is useful when checking whether dormice or wood mice are visiting artificial nest sites, as both sometimes take such stones inside to open. The holes in these small stones when opened by dormice are so neat that they can look as if they were made by a fine drill.

Even immature dormice readily open sloe stones. This refutes the generally held view that dormouse jaws are only strong enough to open hazel nuts before they are fully ripe – it is only at that stage that the nuts are still attached to the tree. I can verify that dormice have strong teeth: an angry dormouse is not to be trifled with, but fortunately they rarely seem inclined to bite, unlike other small rodents.

Although dormice are traditionally linked to hazel coppice, hazel nuts are not essential to dormice, and even where present are not always eaten by them. Eaten hazel nuts may be an accurate method of checking for dormouse presence and the easiest field sign to find, but it can only be used where there are fruiting hazel trees. Even where fruiting hazel is abundant, I have found it can be extremely difficult, even after years of searching, to find dormouse eaten nuts. Not only have I nearly always found woodlands to be one of the hardest habitats in which to find dormouse eaten nuts, but also I have found areas where the nuts are abundant in a wood to be especially difficult. This I do not attribute merely to the number of nuts to check (fortunately dormouse eaten nuts usually land hole side uppermost), but to the fact that an abundance of nuts seems to attract more competition, especially in the form of grey squirrels, which often take most of the nuts before they have even started to ripen, leaving none for the dormice.

I have had more success in finding dormouse eaten nuts in the parts of a wood where few nuts are produced, or where the hazel was not in a wood. This is probably due to squirrels

above: Hazel nuts opened by dormice

opposite: Hazel nuts opened by wood mice

Living with Dormice

not being so attracted to habitats where hazel nuts are less numerous. In one wood I despaired of finding dormouse eaten nuts, but quickly found one in an adjacent hedgerow. On a couple of occasions in other hedgerows I found that a dormouse had opened the very first nut I came across!

When initially I did a survey in western Dorset, I searched for dormice wherever I found fruiting hazel. This is a scantily wooded area compared with most of southern England, but has a good network of hedges. I looked at a range of habitats and chiefly targeted areas away from woodland. Many of the sites had no significant area of woodland within a 2-3km radius, and some were 4km or more from a wood of 10 or more hectares.[1] Over most of western Dorset hazel is abundant but it is difficult to find fruiting hazel, owing to modern hedgerow management. Bottoms of hedgerows are not generally as congenial as woodlands to search for nuts because of the dense undergrowth, including ivy, which does not die down in winter, and to the dumping of rubbish. I know very well what it is like to come out of a hedge backwards – and one can get some funny looks! It is not surprising that mainly woodland has been targeted in the past.

Over the winter of 1998-99 I checked some fifty-two sites, where I found at least fifty nuts eaten by some species of mammal. I failed to find dormouse eaten nuts at only four sites. Subsequently I have been able to show that there are indeed dormice at three of these sites. The only remaining site was alongside a lay-by and finding eaten nuts among the rubbish was a feat in itself, which I did not care to repeat. One of the sites that I returned to was on the chalklands north of Dorchester. In this area of mainly arable farming, the farmers tend to flail the hedgerows to near extinction, so there seemed no alternative other than to look in one of the few scattered woods. The wood I checked was about 10ha in size and only about 2km away from a wood where I already knew there were dormice. After two visits looking through carpets of hundreds of nuts with only negative results, Jan Crowden, came to the rescue. Both she and her husband are experienced nut hunters, and by targeting an area, which I had previously not checked, they found a dormouse eaten nut. It had taken a total of nine hours hunting to prove that there were dormice in that wood! Nevertheless hunting for that nut eaten by a dormouse was probably the most efficient and least time consuming way of proving that dormice were present.

So remember that patience is needed, but will probably be best rewarded in areas where there are not too many nuts. Any piles of nuts near the trunks of hazel bushes are most likely to have been collected by wood mice. Dormice open most nuts *in situ*, out on the branches, so the majority fall well away from the trunks.

Surveying for Dormice

Searching for dormouse nests

Searching for summer nests used to be thought a good way of locating areas occupied by dormice. In the first national survey, records of dormouse presence were from a whole range of habitats, including gardens, bramble thickets and young plantations.[1] The wide range of habitats cited is due to the majority of records coming from finds of nests rather than eaten hazel nuts. Since then, searching for nests has been neglected and surveys are based only on searches for eaten hazel nuts, which are easier to find than nests. This is unfortunate because dormice live in many habitats where hazel is absent. Through searching for nests I have obtained some of my most useful evidence into their habitats, which can be so very different from those described previously. Also, nests have shown me just how widespread and how common dormice are, even in areas far away from any woodland. Nests are a good method of obtaining records of dormouse presence and can produce useful results. But this method has major constraints as dormice usually hide their summer nests so well that they can be almost impossible to find.

Over the years I have come to realise that the possibility of actually finding summer nests can depend greatly on the habitat and the structure of the vegetation, as it is only in certain places that dormice are likely to build nests that are at all easy to find. Previous methods of nest hunting have used a garden rake or similar tool, so as to be able to access the interior of bramble patches. This is a rather destructive and time intensive method, and if used in summer would be very disruptive to the dormice, and would indeed be unlawful. As nests are almost impossible to see before the leaves have fallen in the autumn, I wait until winter. I have had little success in woodland, but there are more hiding places there, and radio tracking has found that few nests are in the understorey where people might find them. Most are up in the trees, in holes or behind loose bark where they are most unlikely to be found. Nests in woods may need to be well hidden from such predators as squirrels and nests hidden from such animals as squirrels are hardly likely to be found very often by the likes of us! It is surprising that dormice often build their nests in the outer layers of squirrels' dreys. Indeed I once found that they had been nesting in a squirrel drey, only feet away from an empty nest box. Dormouse nests are so frequently reported from squirrels' dreys, that dreys could indeed prove to be rewarding places to search in woods for dormouse nests.

A nest hidden among ivy – a difficult place to search

Nests are most likely to be found in low scrub and bramble patches. Searches there can be quite rewarding, but it can be time consuming and physically difficult to search through bramble and gorse thickets. Nests are often so well hidden that other approaches may be useful. Working parties clearing scrub could perhaps be asked to look out for nests. A friend was recently clearing an area of gorse off chalk grassland, and I had more than one phone call asking what to do with hibernating dormice found in nests among the stools of the gorse. More records of dormouse

above: Summer nests of dormice can be very obvious in winter, after the leaves have fallen, but most nests are much better hidden

presence could be obtained if people involved in such land management as hedging, coppicing, scrub clearance and even gardening were aware of the significance of small spherical woven nests. One couple I met had been gardening and had placed three nests on a rubbish pile ready for burning assuming they were just old mouse nests. The following weekend, curiosity induced them to examine the nests more closely, and they found they contained hibernating dormice.

The hedges and scrub on the seaward facing hillsides above the Chesil Bank are where I have had most success in finding summer nests. The hedges are not managed regularly and thus provide the habitat structure where dormice will anchor their nests in relatively easily visible places. Obvious nests are often right on the outside of hedges and scrub in relatively new, much branched, stems of blackthorn, and in bramble patches. Such nests are positioned in seemingly insecure places, often with much better developed scrub nearby. This I can only surmise is because they have chosen sites less likely to be frequented by other rodents. More often nests are hidden in the densest and easiest vegetation around for anchorage. Gorse bushes are favoured, and in this coastal area they often choose swags of wild madder, a large relative of goosegrass, which has a chiefly coastal distribution in the South-West and Wales. The chance of finding nests in the scrub in our garden has increased since we planted some wild madder; three of the four nests I found one year were in one small area of madder.

Many nests are so obvious when the leaves have fallen that I tend not to spend time disturbing the vegetation. Just searching along local footpaths one winter I found over sixty nests, and the following winter, with less effort but increasing awareness of the best habitat to search, over

above: Summer dormouse nest in young dog wood scrub where a whorl of twigs makes an anchorage for a nest

Surveying for Dormice

eighty. In fact, winter dormouse nests appeared to far outnumber bird nests in the area. Bird nests are always worth checking for dormouse nests: I have found one in the cup of a thrush's nest as well as one woven inside a wren's nest. It seemed that it was only during the last few winters that I had really got my eye in for finding dormouse nests. However, my last hunt after the summer of 2006 has made me think again. It was in the winter of 2005-6 that I found over eighty nests in the coastal area near my home, whereas the following winter I found far fewer. On reflection it seems that it is significant that my most successful nest hunting coincided with years when there had been large populations of wood mice in the area, whereas in the summer of 2006 the wood mouse populations crashed. It seems that more dormouse nests may be built and more positioned in extreme positions when wood mice are in greater numbers and are harassing the dormice more. I have found with nest boxes that wood mice take over dormouse nests and will kill dormice when they are in torpor. It does though still remain a puzzle as to where dormice are hiding most of their nests.

> nests hidden from predators such as squirrels are hardly likely to be found by the likes of us!

Over the years I have been progressively looking for and finding nests in more and more seemingly extreme situations. Having now found nests in low, salt-battered scrub, barely one metre from a footpath on the shingle of the beach, where can I look next? I have also been astounded by the number of nests I have found in the hedgerows bordering the relatively busy road leading into our village. One winter I found a dozen along the 1.5km length of hedgerows, even though the hedges are often flailed and have many gaps including several long lengths of just wire fencing. What was even more surprising was that some were so close to the road; all were within 2.5m of the road, three within one metre and one, only 50cm above ground level, was just 30cm in from the edge of the tarmac.

Unfortunately most hedges further inland are managed every year and they tend to be flailed before leaf-fall so many of the nests (and young dormice) will be lost before they are ever visible. In one hedgerow, which had been flailed along one side only, I found a nest anchored in the taller uncut side. This kind of intense management tends to remove the structural elements in a hedge where nests are likely to be found, and more inland hedges are draped with ivy compared with the coastal hedges, making visibility into many hedgerows almost nil. I have found fewer nests in the hedgerows further inland, but have only carried out a far more limited number of searches there. I have, though, been successful in finding a nest on most visits, which indicates a very widespread presence of dormice in these hedgerows, often far from any woodland.

Summer nest in a gorse bush. Not the easiest place to find nests, but such dense vegetation is often chosen by dormice

Numbers of dormouse nests can never be equated to numbers of dormice, as dormice build and use several nests during their active season. As the majority of nests are so well hidden, a habitat would usually have to be completely dissected to find them all. In our own blackthorn scrub, where nest boxes tell me that dormice are around, only occasionally have I ever managed to find nests built in the bushes. In the autumn of 2004, when I found and marked twenty-five dormice in the nest boxes, I found only three wild nests. In other sites inland where I have dormice using nest boxes, I have had even more difficulty in finding wild nests. I heard about a good example of nest concealment in Devon. A hedge that was being moved for road widening appeared to have no nests however hard and from whatever angle it was searched. It was only when it was being dug up that nests were found near the base. Similarly, I heard of dormice being observed in a large cage, where they were thought to have been breeding. But the nest was found only once the young emerged, as it was hidden at ground level, not up in the bushes as expected.

It does indeed seem that the most certain way of locating dormouse presence in any habitat is by looking for nests when it is being managed. Dormice were very loath to use nest boxes in one wood and I gave up in one part of it. However, when the area was subsequently coppiced over a dozen dormouse nests were found in about one hectare. At the Swannery in Abbotsbury (see Appendix), coppicing of only a small area of willow carr produced six dormouse nests, whereas it had taken seven years using artificial nesting sites to prove dormice were there.

Dormouse summer nest built where wild madder is scrambling up a hedge

Surveying for Dormice

Providing artificial nesting sites for dormice

Dormice are so elusive that they are rarely seen unless they are trapped or found in artificial nesting sites. It was only in the 1980s that studies of dormice in the wild were started in earnest in Britain. This was when Doug Woods found that dormice would use wooden nest boxes for breeding and shelter during the summer months.[1] Nest boxes have since been used as the main method for studying dormouse populations. They can be a good method for seeing dormice, but are not a robust enough method for monitoring them. More recently, nest tubes have been used for some surveys. In some habitats tubes appear more attractive to dormice than do boxes, but again care is needed in the interpretation of results. The factors influencing the use of both boxes and tube by dormice appear to have been sadly overlooked.

Nest boxes for dormice

After weighing, dormice are 'posted' back into their box

The nest boxes used for monitoring dormice are almost identical to those used for hole nesting birds such as tits, but with the entrance hole of 35mm in diameter at the back facing the tree trunk. Spacing bars above and below the entrance hole keep the box clear of the trunk. The idea is that with the hole at the back, dormice can get in easily but birds not so easily. In practice it does not keep birds out and dormice do not mind the position of the hole. On the Continent bird boxes with front entrances have been used to study dormice, and boxes with front holes are just as liked by dormice and far easier to use when working in habitats with brambles. It is said that boxes should be placed 1.5-2m off the ground as this is the height preferred by dormice, and that boxes higher up are not more likely to be used. It does make checking easier, but studies at some sites have shown that dormice actually prefer boxes placed higher.[1] The boxes are suspended in a loop of wire, so that they can be easily removed and placed in a large plastic bag before the lids are removed. Any dormice present can thus be caught, weighed, sexed and perhaps marked. Ringing with aluminium rings, or toe amputations have been used to mark animals on the Continent. In Britain tattooing ears or fur clipping have been the preferred methods, and with improved technology, implanted microchips are now being used. Fur clipping is a simple and useful method, but the dormice grow new fur before hibernation so the clip can rarely be seen the following season.

Living with Dormice

Nest boxes are at present the main method used for "monitoring" dormouse populations. At least fifty and in some places several hundred boxes are located at over 150 sites in association with the National Dormouse Monitoring Programme. The conclusions drawn from this programme are discussed in a later section. Here I would like to point out some of the flaws that I have found with using boxes for "monitoring" dormice. For those interested, and perhaps involved in monitoring dormice, a summary of many of my own results, together with the problems encountered and significance of these, is to be found in the Appendix.

Nest boxes are a good way of being able (if lucky) to see dormice and to show them to other people, but not as a method of monitoring them. This is primarily due to competition for the boxes with other rodents and birds. Dormice are not reliant on holes in trees for their nests, as are such birds as tits, but do seem to prefer them to other sites when competition is absent. However, rather than being safe places for dormice, nest boxes can be dangerous traps, as they have only a single escape hole. Boxes stand out like sore thumbs in most habitats, making any nests more easily found by such predators as weasels. A torpid dormouse in a box is a sitting target; all too often even wood mice will readily kill dormice in torpor. Dormice avoid using boxes in areas where competition with other box-using rodents is high and this is probably the chief regulator in controlling dormouse use of boxes.

Nest box hung on hazel at Kingcombe. In most habitats they stand out and predators may home in on them

On one of my sites with clay soil, which tends to flood in the winter, the boxes were so appreciated by the wood mice that they virtually excluded all dormice. That there were plenty of dormice in the area was shown by the use of nest tubes, which dormice took to very readily. One year at this same site the activities of a weasel produced a year without any sign of a dormouse anywhere near a box. On my two sites in coastal scrub, competition with wood mice is also high, and the dormice that use the boxes are nearly all juveniles either found early in the season, or in autumn after storms have removed most of the leaves from the bushes. On both of these sites a brood of young was found with teeth marks indicating that they had been killed by wood mice. In over ten years only one brood of healthy young has ever been found in a nest box on the two sites, but plenty of grown young are found in the autumn on these sites, showing that the dormice have been breeding in their own wild nests.

The site where I have had most boxes, and still have fifty to comply with the National Dormouse Monitoring Programme, is inland on the Kingcombe Meadows Reserve of the Dorset Wildlife Trust. Here some of the boxes are in areas of scrub, some composed mainly of hazel, and some in hedgerows (see Appendix for more details). Here, fewer wood mice use the boxes, but they still appear to be the controlling factor in dormouse use of the boxes. Initially I thought that dormice were ignoring the boxes in areas where there appeared to be more possible natural nesting sites, but I gradually realised that these were areas with more undergrowth and areas where wood mice used more of the boxes. West Dorset is at the western limit of distribution of the yellow-necked mouse, and only in some years did it make an appearance at Kingcombe. The yellow-necked mouse is more arboreal in habit than the wood mouse and as well as using boxes in the hedges, tended to use boxes on hazel trees, in areas where there was little undergrowth and so generally avoided by wood mice. In these years dormouse use of the boxes was consequently even lower.

The boxes are hung on wire loops so they can be lifted off and put into polythene bags, allowing the dormice to be caught

Surveying for Dormice 73

Populations of wood mice, like most rodents, fluctuate greatly from year to year. Although I have no absolute measurement of the wood mouse populations, the apparent size of their populations was generally inversely proportional to the number of boxes used by dormice. In 2005, when wood mice and yellow-necked mice were most abundant at Kingcombe, numbers of dormice recorded were at their lowest: in October only three dormice were seen in over sixty boxes. Populations of these other mice crashed in 2006, and record numbers of dormice used the boxes: in October thirty-five dormice were seen in fifty boxes, and yet more were in nest tubes in the same area. If population changes really were being shown by dormouse use of boxes, such population fluctuations would not be expected in an animal that produces relatively few young. It was ten years of checking boxes on this site before such a massive crash in other mouse numbers occurred: one needs to have patience to study dormice!

I have carried out some preliminary experiments to try and ascertain other factors that affect dormouse use of boxes. Seeding boxes with bedding material encourages more dormice to use them. I am cautious about advocating widespread use of such methods, as it may just be tempting dormice into dangerous situations. I have carried out only small-scale experiments, as seeding is also appreciated by wood mice, and hence could be encouraging dormice to use unsafe nesting sites. But then I do not really approve of the widespread use of nest box schemes, as boxes anywhere may be providing nesting sites that are more dangerous for dormice than are natural sites. Surprisingly the results from 2006, when wood mouse numbers crashed, indicate that an important factor was that bedding tended to keep birds, especially tits, from breeding or roosting in the boxes. This is despite dormice often seeming to take over nests started by tits. These experiments are discussed in greater detail in the Appendix. The limited experiments that I have carried out with bedding added, or comparisons with tubes, have shown that many factors need to be considered and boxes should not be accepted as an infallible method of monitoring dormice. On the Continent a host of competitors for dormouse nest boxes have been documented, and dormouse nests left from the previous year were found to have a negative impact on breeding birds such as tits.[2]

Experimenting in a woodland with different sized nest boxes placed at different heights up trees. All the boxes ended up with wood mice in them!

It does seem that the pleasure of even occasionally seeing a dormouse keeps hundreds of surveyors at the task, year after year. I can probably be counted as guilty here, but I have cut boxes at one site to the minimum required to stay in the programme, and at the other sites I have more or less changed over to nesting tubes, which will be discussed in the next section. Although dormice at times seem to like boxes, there appears to have been little experimentation to find which artificial nesting containers suit them best. In my experience they do not behave to order. One can only smile at a report of a box site where a nest and live dormouse were found in an old polythene bag one year, but the dormice did not use any of the nest boxes.[3]

It has often been said that trapping small mammals is as much an art as a science. Positioning nest boxes (and tubes) seems to be in the same category. It is surprising that so much effort is put into checking boxes when results are often so dire, and that nest boxes are still accepted as such an infallible way of studying dormice. A little bit more thought on the matter might produce more dormice using the boxes, at least in some years, and give a better indication as to how common they are. Dormice like dry, clean, and hence well-maintained boxes. It really does seem pointless that hundreds of boxes are put out and then left to gradually rot. Boxes should be brought in each winter for cleaning and mending. I do not claim that I always do this, but I have reduced the number of boxes on some sites, as results from a few well maintained boxes can be just as good as from a large number of old, damp boxes.

Very high usage of boxes by dormice is at times due to new, clean boxes, which are therefore untainted by other rodents. One site that I have visited, where new boxes produced large numbers of dormice, was in a plantation of twenty-year-old Corsican pine. By October of the first year twenty-nine of the fifty boxes had dormice nests and thirty-five dormice were seen. During the first year only one box was recorded as being used by wood mice, and that was not until October. By April of the next year wood mice were resident in sixteen of the boxes and subsequently only a handful of them were used by dormice, bringing the results down to the normal low levels generally obtained from most nest box schemes.

Numbers of dormice using nest boxes are at times better if boxes are placed higher than suggested, so that they are in the leafy feeding zone of the trees (or encourage your local bat group to put up boxes – dormice are not at all averse to bat boxes). Or do as I often do, forget boxes in woods and try nesting tubes in hedges and scrub. I hope I can give a little more optimism to the many who struggle on year after year with few if any dormice in their boxes. It is probably because dormice choose safer places away from other rodents. Many of the factors involved in their choosing to use boxes are still not understood. Dormice can be extremely fickle when it comes to using boxes, thus making boxes a hopeless way of measuring their populations. This fickleness is well illustrated in a report of two nest box schemes in two ecologically similar woods near Carmarthen. Twenty boxes were set up in each wood; at one site the boxes were quickly used and three families were seen by July of the first year; the boxes in the other wood produced their first dormouse eleven years later, although eaten hazelnuts and summer nests proved that dormice were there!

Dormice have rarely been reported from nest boxes put up for birds. This may be partly due to bird boxes often being positioned on trunks of trees remote from leafy areas, but also because those checking the boxes do not realise that they may get dormouse nests and do not know what to look for. Usually by the time most bird nest boxes are cleaned out, the dormice will have gone into hibernation elsewhere, and wood mice may have trashed the nests. However, since I have shown dormouse nests to a friend, he has brought me pictures of dormouse nests in his bird boxes. One major exception to few records of dormice being found was in Gordon Vaughan's bird boxes in Devon.[4] Several features of his nest box scheme made it attractive to dormice, but primarily they were placed high up in the trees. The boxes, compared with a standard dormouse box, were "incorrectly" made with a hole on the outside surrounded by a wide metal strip – to deter squirrels – and were creosoted, but on the plus side the boxes were very well maintained being clean and dry inside. Another factor that may have helped Gordon achieve such good results was that he put the boxes in clusters of three, so that the tits would not take over all the boxes before the pied flycatchers arrived back from Africa. Boxes placed at 20m intervals, as is normal with dormouse boxes, are distant enough to allow tits to acquire most of them without territorial disputes. So the clustering of his boxes may have also helped the dormice by providing tit free boxes. Unfortunately, the dormice often took over flycatchers' nests, which are often made largely of honeysuckle bark, hence providing instant nest material for dormice. I do not remember him saying that they ever took over the nests of tits: great tits especially can be quite formidable opponents, whereas flycatchers seem far less aggressive.

After nine years the first dormouse found in a box at Abbotsbury Swannery was in this box, which had been changed into a tit box. Several years earlier, when it was still a 'dormouse box' wood mice bred in it

Nesting tubes for dormice

Nesting tubes are a relatively new method for surveying dormice. They consist of a length of square sectioned tubing, made of lightweight, black corrugated plastic, 25cm long and 6.5cm wide. A wooden tray is slotted inside, which extends at one end well beyond the opening, but the tube is blocked by a piece of wood at the other end. They are hung horizontally under suitable branches. Tubes have the advantage of being relatively cheap and easily transported. They are useful when looking for the presence of dormice, but have disadvantages for long-term studies of dormice. It is difficult to capture dormice in tubes, because they usually manage to shoot out before one can get near the tube. This is probably due to the lack of any soundproofing compared with a box made of thick wood. Annoyingly it is easier to catch wood mice in tubes, as they tend to sit tight for longer. A licence is required if the dormice in the tubes are to be disturbed and handled. In most habitats wood mice prefer to usurp dormouse nests in tubes rather than build their own from scratch. It is dubious if nesting tubes are of help to dormice, and they can be traps with only a single exit; as I have unfortunately been able to verify: a scalped dormouse is not a pretty sight.

A small square tube produces a small square nest, which for the beginner is not as easily diagnosed as a round nest in a box. It is usually in the form of a well-structured tubular nest, whereas wood mice create an untidy, chewed up layer, with no roof to it, even when they have taken over a dormouse nest. The material used by dormice for nest building has been said to be diagnostic, but this is not so. With nest tubes especially, it is amazing what they will use; they obviously grab anything at hand so they are out in the open for the shortest possible time. I have known them to use thistledown, thistle leaves, and stinging nettle leaves! The thistle down especially puzzled me, but fortunately the nest was subsequently given a beautifully woven grass lining. Unfortunately a large wood mouse wrecked it before I could congratulate the original builder.

I was first introduced to nest tubes through the South West Dormouse Project launched by Michael Woods and Paul Chanin with a view to using nest tubes to find how widespread dormice are in the South West, and in what sort of habitat they occur, as they were being recorded in all sorts of "non-typical" or "odd" habitats. They also wished to see if they could devise a reliable protocol to determine the presence or absence of dormice where there was no fruiting hazel. Anyone wanting to use tubes should read their report.[1] Volunteers installed tubes at over a hundred sites. Dormice were subsequently recorded at thirty-two sites covering all the main habitat types tested, including coniferous woodland, scrub associated with culm grassland, heavily managed hedges, gorse, birch scrub, and coastal scrub. This project confirmed that dormice are found in a much wider range of habitats than just species rich woodlands and hedgerows. It also showed that with such a method of surveying, negative results should not be assumed to mean that there are no dormice present, as dormice were known to be present at eight sites where they did not use the tubes. At one such site the dormouse even found the surveyor by leaping onto her neck! It did not seem to matter to which species of shrub the tube was attached. Nest tubes on bramble were found to

above: Tubes are delivered flat-packed. They consist of an inner wooden tray and an outer plastic tube. They can be obtained from the Mammal Society

above: Tubes are best hung on the outer twigs of bushes

opposite: Tube with the plastic outer tube removed to show a dormouse nest made of grass

76   *Living with Dormice*

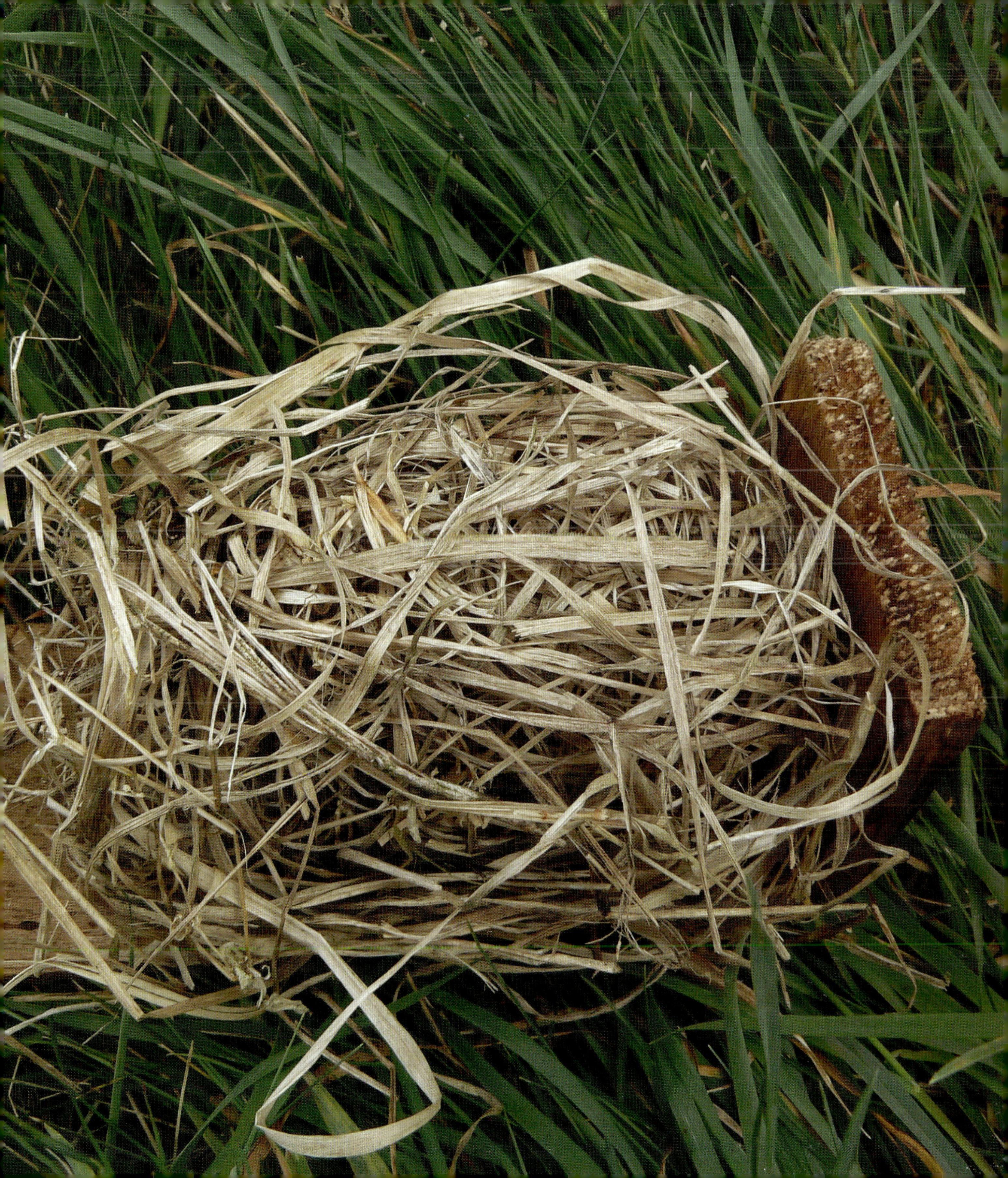

work well, but the growth rate of bramble can make relocation of the tubes almost impossible. However, there was a difference in usage of tubes in different habitats.

Tubes seemed to work well in scrub and hedgerows, and in coniferous woodland, but poor results were obtained in most deciduous woodland, the classical habitat for dormice. I had no success with nesting tubes on the one occasion that I tried them in deciduous woodland, whereas I had instant success in a nearby hedge. It may be that tubes are rather inferior nesting sites compared with natural sites in deciduous woodland, or it could be that tubes are too obvious and accessible to predators such as grey squirrels. Possibly it could be that the tubes need to be positioned more at the tops of the trees in the denser leafy zones, rather than just in positions that can be reached from ground level by the monitors.

> nests have even been made from **thistle** and stinging nettle leaves

Nesting tubes are best attached to the branches with wire. I do not recommend string, having seen this result in a string nest inside the tube! Most people attach the tubes directly to the branches, so that they do not move relative to the branch. I twist the wire onto the tube and then onto the branch, so the tubes can be removed more easily without losing the wires. Despite the tubes seeming very unstable in any wind, this method has worked well, even in windswept coastal scrub.

Having used tubes for several years now, I find that their positioning can be critical. When I first saw the tubes I was very dubious as to whether dormice would ever use them. I was all for tucking them away in the centre of bushes, but fortunately I was ill and Roy put up our first tubes. He placed them out in March on the outer branches of the bushes, in very exposed positions, so that he could easily retrieve them. Even before the leaves were out, he found dormice in some of them. Having used tubes for several years, I find that tubes are indeed more likely to be used if they are put in the green leafy parts of thin branches. It was probably significant that, when checking a set of tubes one July, the only tube with a dormouse actually in it, was in such an exposed position that it was the only tube not buried by new growth. In hedgerows I have had good results by just hanging the tubes on the wire fences that protect the hedges from being browsed by farm animals. It is possible that sites on the extremities of bushes are less attractive to wood mice, and hence safer for dormice. Although tubes on the extremities of bushes seem to attract most dormice, they do need to be adjacent to thick tangles of leafy vegetation. Finding good accessible sites for tubes, where there are suitable horizontal supports, can be difficult in many habitats, and may be why tubes fail in so many places. Unfortunately a drawback to putting tubes in exposed positions is that they are more easily noticed by any casual passer-by, and as their function is not obvious they are more likely than nest boxes to be investigated.

It seems therefore that the results from putting up tubes can be useful in locating the presence of dormice. But just as with nest boxes, negative results must not be taken to mean that dormice are not present, nor can they be used as a measure of population size. It seems that dormice rarely consider tubes or nest boxes as the prime or safest locations. Both are used more in spring and autumn, rather than during the main breeding season, and chiefly by animals under a year old, who are more inexperienced. In hedgerows and scrub I find dormice generally more likely to use tubes than nest boxes probably because of the competition with wood mice for sites. Wood mice prefer the shelter provided by a box rather than the openness of a tube. However, wood mice will build nests in tubes but seem to prefer them

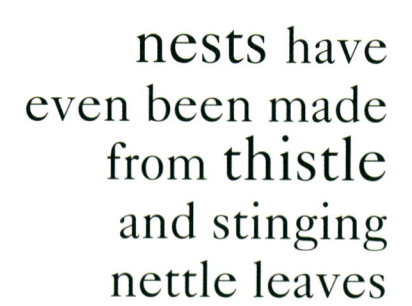

Tube hanging on a hawthorn twig in Salway Ash Churchyard. The tray has been pulled out far enough to show the dormouse nest inside

Living with Dormice

when dormice have built there first. Wood mice should be considered as arborealists far more than they are generally given credit for. It is surprising how at times they take to tubes: I have found them in groups of up to four, in tubes some 1.5m above ground level where they were being buffeted by the slightest breeze. In such situations there is often more mouse than bedding in the tube.

Nesting tubes form a useful additional surveying method, but like other methods should not be used as a universal panacea, even for locating the presence of dormice. If conditions are such that dormice will use tubes, in no way can the number of tubes be related to population size. More tubes may be used where wood mice are taking over the dormouse nests, as often the dormice then relocate to other vacant tubes.

It may be possible to devise better artificial nesting sites for dormice, which would be less wood mouse friendly. I have yet to experiment much along these lines. When I did put two pseudo birds' nests made of hay in the frames of old hanging baskets with the tops covered to keep them dry, I did end up with two dormouse nests. This could be tried in garden hedges, and I suspect that they might be more readily used than nest boxes in some situations. Variations on nest tubes could easily be devised. I tried making a couple of tubes out of canvas, about the same dimensions as a nesting tube but open at both ends, and was soon rewarded by a dormouse nest.

above: Even stinging nettles can be dragged into a tube to make a nest

below: Dormice nests from tubes. The two inner nests show the tubular nests typical of dormice. The two outer nests have been trashed by wood mice, who take over dormice nests rather than build their own

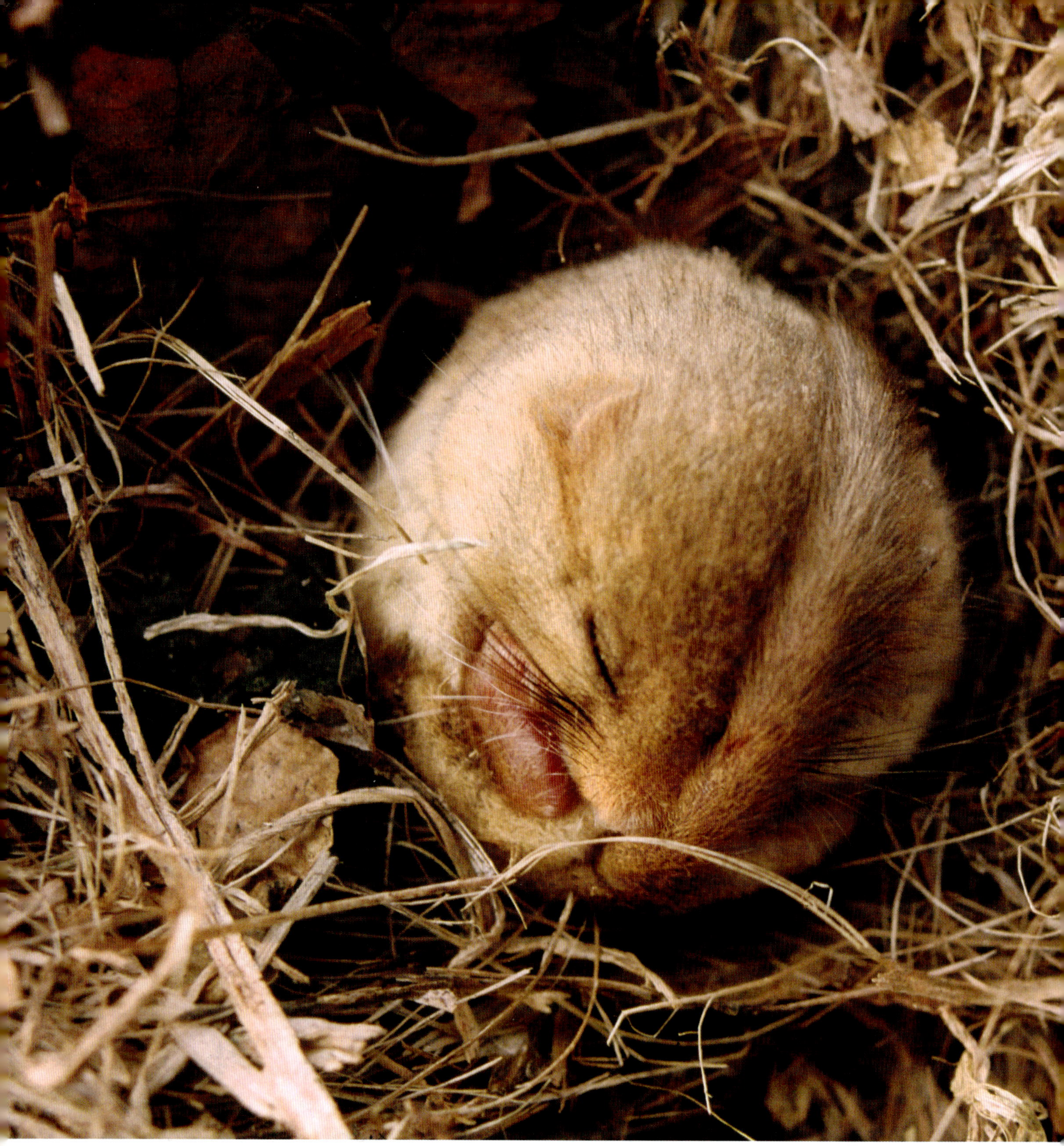

Other studies on dormice in Britain

Dormice are such elusive animals that little had been found out about their lives in Britain, and little was written about them, except for a few short articles and local natural history society reports, before the latter part of the last century. Reports from the late nineteenth and early twentieth centuries say that dormice were to be found in almost every county in England and Wales. Where there was plenty of undergrowth, they were reported as common in England south of the Midlands, widely but locally distributed in Wales, the western English counties and much of northern England, but rare in the Midlands and parts of East Anglia.

Elaine Hurrell carried out some of the first field studies near her home in Devon, and wrote two small booklets on dormice.[1] She concluded from her work that dormice prefer to live in places where there is plenty of undergrowth, and that woodland is not suitable for dormice where trees are of mature growth with less undergrowth. She was in agreement with others that the dormouse was much scarcer than in previous generations and suggested that an important factor could be the reduction in coppicing of hazel. Her father observed their captive dormice and realised that they opened hazel nuts in a distinctive way. This new way of finding evidence of dormice made possible the first national survey of dormice in the 1970s, and Elaine helped organise it for the Mammal Society.[2] The results of the survey seemed to agree with the general thinking of the time that the dormouse had become much scarcer than it had been at the start of the century, and may even have disappeared from seven counties in the north and Midlands, where it occurred only a hundred years before.

The dormouse, because of its perceived rarity, has been given legal protection. The then Nature Conservancy Council (now part of Natural England) wanted to know why the dormouse was so rare and what, if anything, could be done about it. Dr Pat Morris of Royal Holloway (University of London) had started to devise methods for studying dormice and in 1984 began looking at these problems, so that scientifically based advice on conservation management could be provided to save dormice from dying out altogether. A method of seeing dormice was needed if more was to be learnt about them; wire mesh traps were first used, but catches were too low to be reliable. He then met up with Doug Woods, a naturalist from Somerset, who had devised a nest box scheme in the hazel woodlands of the Cheddar Gorge. This gave a method of regularly seeing and catching enough dormice to study.

Because the dormouse is so elusive, little was previously known about its way of life. Before 1985 there appear to have been only two scientific papers published about British dormice, and little was known of their ecology.[2,3] Since 1985 nearly all publications in Britain about dormice are based on the work of Dr Pat Morris, Dr Paul Bright (who undertook much of the pioneering fieldwork) and their team based at Royal Holloway. In addition to their various academic studies, they coordinated several nut hunts. Their studies with nest boxes led to the National Dormouse Monitoring Programme, where they organised the collection of data from nest boxes in various parts of the country. Between 150 and 200 sites with nest boxes are now checked each year in this scheme.

The conclusion drawn from their work is that the dormouse is a rare animal, whose range in Britain has decreased by 50 per cent over the past hundred years. They claim that their research has revealed reasons for the rarity and decline of the dormouse, and has established a sound scientific basis for a national recovery programme. They state that the dormouse has specialised food requirements, needing a continuous supply of arboreal flowers and fruits during its active season, with hazel nuts or similar fruits essential for fattening up before hibernation. They suggest that such requirements are seldom met except in ancient woodland, and such woodland needs management in the form of coppicing and removal of "excess" standard trees if the dormouse is to survive. Their conclusions have been accepted as the "official" edict on dormice by such authorities as English Nature (now part of Natural England); many authorities are following their ideas for conservation management for dormice. Their work, therefore, is worth detailed deliberation. Their conclusions have been well documented and on the surface appear conclusive and believable. I am not attempting to review all their literature here. Of the reams of papers and booklets that they have produced about dormice, summaries of their work are probably, for the more general reader, best found in the following: *Dormice* by Pat Morris (2004), *The Dormouse* by Paul Bright and Pat Morris (2005), *The Dormouse Conservation Handbook* by Paul Bright, Pat Morris and Tony Mitchell-Jones (2005), and for those who would like slightly more in depth coverage, the review paper *Why are Dormice rare? A case study in conservation biology* (Bright and Morris 1996).

In my early years of looking at dormice, I found it difficult not to believe what was published in authoritative journals and handbooks. I now query many of the findings of the work carried out at Royal Holloway, and consider the dormouse far too elusive an animal to be amenable to many of the studies undertaken. I do not agree with many of their conclusions about the dormouse, and I query some of the logic they have used. Most of the conservation efforts based on their conclusions seem misplaced, but fortunately the dormouse just carries on in its own inimitable way. There is, of course, still much to be found out about this elusive animal.

> the dormouse, because of its perceived rarity, has been given legal protection

A Mad Hatter's tea party?

The team at Royal Holloway claim the dormouse has exacting ecological requirements, which render it very vulnerable to extinction. They suggest that extinctions are caused by such factors as fragmentation, deterioration and loss of specialised habitats, combined with the dormouse's low population density and low reproductive rate. These are said to make the dormouse susceptible to the climatic variability of Britain. It is thought that there have been piecemeal, but progressive extinctions, particularly in the northern parts of its range in Britain, but also in their heartlands in the south.

The range of the dormouse in Britain is held to be contracting southwards. They now categorically state that over the past hundred years dormice have become extinct across half their range in England, having disappeared from large areas of the Midlands and the north.[1] Even in the southern part of the range, where the dormouse is held to be reasonably secure, they conclude that "most woods do not contain dormice and the species seems to be distributed very patchily."[2] Over all of its range they conclude that it is so scarce, and so patchily distributed, local extinctions will inevitably occur.

In seeking reasons for the demise of the dormouse, the main conclusions are summarised in the following passage: "The answer probably lies in the dormouse's specialist lifestyle and strict dependence on woodland. The once-extensive wildwood that covered Britain has been reduced to isolated woods, often separated by intensively farmed land which dormice are unable to cross easily. This fragmentation is probably the key reason for the decline of the dormouse, though the effect has been compounded by the loss of connecting hedgerows and the abandonment of traditional coppice management."[3]

It is actually unlikely that such a major decline has occurred and more likely that the elusiveness of the dormouse combined with changes in land management methods, has resulted in few dormice being seen. None of the methods used for surveying for dormice can compare with the Victorian woodmen working by hand, day after day, in the woods. It took me seven years of checking nest boxes and tubes at the Swannery at Abbotsbury, before dormice condescended to use just one nest tube (see Appendix). Subsequently, the coppicing of only a small area of willow carr produced six dormouse nests! Previous conclusions as to the rarity of the dormouse are mainly based on surveys that have major flaws. In addition, the dormouse is held to be a woodland species, so that is virtually the only place where people look for it. I found woodlands one of the harder places in which to find evidence of dormice. By searching sites other than woodland, I found the dormouse to be widespread in West Dorset, and have no reason to believe this is not the case in many other areas, especially in the southern counties of Britain.

The Nut Hunts: finding the distribution of dormice in Britain

Three major national surveys have been carried out, all using hazel nut searches. They were based on the premise that dormice always eat hazel nuts where available, and therefore leave signs of their presence, since hazel nuts are held to be a very important pre-hibernal food source.[1,2]

The Nut Hunt surveys were carried out to assess the changes in distribution and to find out whether the dormouse had survived in areas where it had been recorded previously. They were mostly based on one-off searches for eaten hazel nuts, mainly carried out by the interested general public. The Great Nut Hunt of 1993 was the largest voluntary wildlife survey ever undertaken in Europe, with over 6,000 people taking part. This survey located 334 sites with dormice in England and Wales.[3] Many other sites were negative and were said to provide the first large-scale confirmation of the disappearance of the dormouse from much of its former range. It was said to confirm that dormice were absent in the seven counties where they could not be found in the earlier Mammal Society survey.[4] The Great Nut Hunt was held to be very successful in finding dormouse sites, as the national Biological Records Centre had received only 52 dormouse records in the previous fifteen years. The number of sites found does seem low though, and it would appear somewhat hasty to accept that the results from such a survey show the definitive distribution of dormice in Britain. Even more surprising when it was also stated that dormice remained widespread in some counties.[5] The survey found only five sites in Herefordshire, whereas a "rigorously" designed stratified survey predicted that dormice still occurred in 34 per cent of the 709 woodland areas in that county.[1]

The Victorian Nut Hunt carried out in 1997 looked at particular sites, especially in the north, where dormice were known to be quite common in Victorian times. The only positive sites were found in the south of the country, and included only 13 per cent of sites known to have dormice in the nineteenth century.[6] This was held to show how serious the decline in dormice had become. A second Great Nut Hunt was carried out in 2001 with the aim of finding new dormouse sites, and to see if dormice were still present at the sites where they were found in 1993. In this survey almost 1,200 people took part and 136 sites were found to have dormice present, 76 of which were sites known from 1993 and 60 were new sites.[7] This was said to have brought the total number of known sites in Britain to over eight hundred. Additional sites, where dormice were detected in 1993, were revisited in 2002, and overall dormouse presence was not detected at 51 per cent of all revisited sites. It was thought that revisiting such sites would indicate the rate at which dormouse populations were being lost locally.[3]

In the national Nut Hunts, casual hunting for nuts was said to be acceptable, but the protocol recommended was "If possible choose an area with lots of hazel and start with a tree with lots of nuts underneath….If you can, spend about twenty minutes looking under each tree or clump of trees. Two hours would be long enough for the whole wood."[8,9] A similar protocol was used when undertaking other surveys using professional staff: areas in woods where hazel was heavily fruiting were chosen and quadrants measuring 10m by 10m were continuously searched for twenty minutes for dormouse eaten nuts. If no nuts eaten by dormice were found, the search effort was terminated after five quadrants had been sampled. If dormouse eaten nuts had not been found in that time it was said that it could be assumed that dormice were absent. Such a systematic search was recommended as it was said that it would be easier to be confident that the failure was due to the absence of dormice rather than accidental failure to find nuts opened by them.[2,9]

Not only are dormice to be found in lots of habitats where hazel is absent, only limited habitats have hazel fruiting abundantly enough to fit the methods suggested. In surveys based on stratified random sampling of woods, woods where hazel was absent or fruiting poorly, were rejected and replaced by woods with abundant fruiting hazel.[2] Such sampling could only magnify the bias in determining dormouse habitat as fruiting hazel in woodland is a characteristic that is largely dependent on coppicing. During the Nut Hunts dormouse sites were rarely found in northern England or in Wales. This is partly due to fewer recorders in these areas, but also to fewer woods with abundant fruiting hazel. When The Vincent Wildlife Trust carried out a survey in Wales they found that the protocol suggested for nut hunts could not be properly deployed in 94 per cent of sites because of the scarcity of fruiting hazel.[10] Even so their survey still found a 70 per cent increase in known 10km squares in Wales where there had been positive evidence of dormouse presence since the 1993 Nut Hunt.

A major problem with the Nut Hunts was that few of the participants had ever seen a dormouse-opened nut. Although distinctive, experience considerably improves hunting success; even some professional ecologists need to be shown nuts several times before they are clear as to what to look for. The methods used in the Nut Hunts would have found some localities where dormice occur, but would also have given too many false negatives. Woodland is often the hardest place in which to find evidence of dormice. The time limit suggested for the searches would often not have been long enough, and dormice do not necessarily eat hazel nuts even when they are present. A major problem with the methodology of the surveys using nuts is that the nut searches were based primarily on areas that had abundant hazel nuts. These areas are the ones most attractive to squirrels, which may leave none for the dormice. They are not the best places to search for dormouse eaten nuts, and are bound to produce many negative results. It is significant that in more recent advice for nut searches it is suggested that where nuts have mostly been opened by squirrels, a further set of areas should be searched before concluding that dormice are absent.[11]

It is not surprising that over 60 per cent of the nuts sent in for checking by helpers in the Great Nut Hunt had been opened by squirrels and only about 10 per cent by dormice. The participants of the Nut Hunts, as well as never having seen nuts opened by dormice, also had to waste time counting all the nuts in the areas that they checked, and this included whole nuts, i.e. those that are left on the ground unopened because they have no contents and are ignored by wildlife. Such nuts accounted for about 25 per cent of the nuts counted.[3] A research report from a student at Royal Holloway even suggested that in one wood, as there were so many whole nuts left under the trees by wintertime, there was plenty of food left for both squirrels and dormice!

National Nut Hunts may be good for involving the general public, but have been poor in returns of knowledge gained. Although useful results have been obtained, such as the first records in Gwynedd for over a hundred years, negative results are too prevalent and should not have been taken as definitive when dealing with such an elusive animal. It is not surprising that dormouse presence was not detected at 51 per cent of all the revisited sites; unfortunately this led to the conclusion that the dormouse distribution in Britain is still rapidly contracting.

A hoard of hazel nuts near the trunk of a hazel bush — the work of wood mice. Dormice usually open nuts in situ on the branches, so the opened nuts are found scattered away from the trunks

Living with Dormice

Nest boxes and the National Dormouse Monitoring Programme

Tree-holes are often used as nesting sites by dormice in woodland. It has even been suggested that a dormouse actually "requires tree holes or other secure nest sites,"[1] and that, "A shortage of good nest holes may be a factor contributing to the species' rarity," and, "A supply of nest boxes helps to provide a good substitute, and almost the entire dormouse population may learn to use them within two years," as, "Here they have protection from the weather and security for their young."[2] This ignores the fact that dormice are often found in habitats where there are no trees to provide any holes. Unlike such birds as tits they are not reliant on holes for nesting, as they often build their nests in the branches of shrubs or among brambles.

The National Dormouse Monitoring Programme developed from work with nest boxes. It began in 1991 and is the longest running single mammal monitoring programme of its kind in Britain.[3] It was set up with the aim of monitoring changes in dormouse abundance, nest boxes providing "an important tool for monitoring numbers and breeding success."[4] The programme is now held to be an effective tool in detecting annual variation in breeding success and changes in population densities. For the past few years it has been run by The People's Trust for Endangered Species in partnership with English Nature (now part of Natural England) and the team at Royal Holloway (University of London). A tremendous amount of effort and expense goes into the National Dormouse Monitoring Programme. Volunteers, who numbered over 600 by the millennium, now survey between 150 and 200 sites each year, which is said to be about 25 per cent of known dormouse sites in Britain. In 2005 records were sent in from 178 sites with a total of 12,787 boxes. At each site at least fifty, but in places several hundred boxes are placed in a grid system in "suitable" woodlands. It is required that the boxes be checked each month from April to November, or at least in June and October, when the dormice are counted, weighed and sexed. The volunteers are trained and have to be licensed, as the dormouse is a protected species. News and preliminary analyses of this work are circulated to the volunteers in a newsletter, *The Dormouse Monitor*.

Through the work using nest boxes, it has been said that the dormouse is now one of Britain's most thoroughly understood small mammals.[5] I disagree. I query the interpretation of the use of boxes by dormice, which is critical in determining their distribution and abundance. Of major significance is that competition for nest boxes with other animals has been virtually ignored. There is no mention of competition with other species of mice and competition with birds such as tits is said not to be significant, as they have fledged before the dormice need the boxes in June.[6]

We are told that if dormice are present they will readily use nest boxes put up for them, and the boxes will provide the dormice with safe and secure homes, even to the extent of increasing their chances of survival. I have found, along with many others, that this is just not the case. It is too simplistic to think that if dormice are present, they will use any boxes put up for them. Such notions imply that the dormouse has few predators or competitors: barely possible for a small rodent living in the real world. Nothing is ever that simple in ecology; species do not live in vacuums. The results from my own nest boxes have shown that competition from wood mice can

A dormouse nest box situated in Kingcombe in an area of mainly hazel, where there is little undergrowth. Dormice often used these boxes, except in years when yellow-necked mice were present

Previous studies on dormice in Britain

virtually exclude dormice from boxes, and boxes can be dangerous places for dormice. Rather than dormouse use of boxes monitoring dormouse populations, it is only the dormouse use of boxes that is being monitored. I have now been using nest boxes for over ten years and I have come to the opposite conclusions to those held by the organisers of the National Dormouse Monitoring Programme as to the usefulness of boxes in studying dormice.

Ignoring the importance of competition with other rodents negates the conclusions that have been derived from nest box monitoring. It also explains why dormouse populations are held to be very low, even in what is said to be prime habitat. Nest boxes cannot be used as a method of determining dormouse populations. They often cannot even be used to determine the actual presence of dormice. When testing for the presence of dormice with nest boxes, absence of dormice has often been assumed after only two or three years of the boxes not being used.[1] Gordon Vaughan had nest boxes up in a wood for eleven years before dormice started using them. In the scrub in our garden, it was six years before dormice started using boxes. Further aims of nest box schemes, such as being able to detect population changes and determine how habitat management affects dormouse abundance, seem even more incredulous. It is dubious that nest boxes ever help dormice. It is probably the removal of most natural nesting sites, and the consequent use of boxes that has led to the assumption that coppicing helps dormice.

Nesting tubes

The conclusions drawn from some surveys using nest tubes generally seem a little hasty.[1] No allowance seems to have been made for a difference in tube usage in different habitats. Also, in the methods used, the tubes were often not checked until after the dormice were thought to have gone into hibernation. This ignores the fact that wood mice readily take over their nests, sometimes even before the dormice have finished building them. Nest tubes need frequent checking if all dormouse nests are to be recognised. In one example of such a survey in a wood, 192 tubes were placed out but only fifteen dormouse nests were found, from which the conclusions were that dormice occurred only in low densities in the wood, and they much preferred the surrounding hedgerows and woodland edges.[2] What would have happened if the tubes in the central parts of the wood had been placed up in the foliage of the trees, rather than low down on leafless branches, which probably were being used as wood mouse highways? Illustrations in most literature show nest tubes attached to fairly sizable branches that look as if they could be such highways. Even in hedgerows the positioning of the tubes appears to be critical. Tubes are not an infallible method of detecting the presence of dormice.

A nest made of thistledown, from inside a nest tube

The numbers game

From the results of the National Dormouse Monitoring Programme, it has been deduced that not only are dormice very rare and thin on the ground, but also the British dormouse population is very small and still decreasing. From analysis of the data from the nest boxes it was announced that numbers of dormice had declined by almost 25 per cent in the first ten years of monitoring. It has also been calculated that a typical population size of dormice is only 3-5 per hectare of woodland, but up to 8-10 adults per hectare in the "best" habitats.[1] In the few known sites in Cumbria and Northumberland, the nest box schemes are said to have shown that the densities of dormice are extremely low, at only 0.47 animals per hectare, and in all these northern sites that there may be fewer than three hundred animals. In 1994 it was believed that dormice numbered only half a million, but it is now considered that this figure was far too high and the current estimate of 45,000 is thought to be closer to the mark, but even this is thought to be shrinking still.[2]

> the estimate for the **British** population of dormice is minute, verging on the mythological

The estimate for the British population of dormice is amazingly minute, verging on the mythological. Even if the 45,000 are divided between only the thousand or so "known" sites, elementary arithmetic, without the help of a computer, is turning the dormouse into a rare phantom. This barely tallies with the twenty-five dormice that I captured and marked one autumn in the patch of scrub in our garden, far from any woodland, or the numbers of dormice that I have found in my other boxes when the pressures from wood mice are lower than usual, or the number of dormice I have been shown at other sites. It is salutary to compare 45,000 with the estimate given for polecats in the same publication. The polecat is a large predator and it is suggested that there could be a similar number in Britain.

The dormouse has been said to be naturally scarce because of low population densities and low recruitment each year, in addition to its specialist habitat requirements. These ideas do not tally with the evidence that I have found. The low population densities given would seem unviable for a small rodent and more like those of a predator. I find it very difficult to accept that a small rodent such as the dormouse, which is vulnerable to so many predators, and competing with so many other rodents in the same habitats, could manage to survive at the population sizes and rates of reproduction that have previously been given. Not only are dormice much more widespread but their real populations must be many times greater than those estimated.

A mathematical approach can be very valuable, but when working with natural populations can be erroneous, because of the need to make basic assumptions, which are not justified by the available data. Population densities and the breeding potential of dormice have been chiefly calculated using data obtained from nest box studies. The evidence from nest boxes is highly contentious, and the low population densities suggested are merely an artefact of accepting results from nest boxes as truly representing the real population, disregarding any reason why dormice might not want to use nest boxes.

The chief overriding factor that deters dormice from using boxes seems to be competition with other rodents. Recent analysis of nest box data has concluded that "dormouse populations vary considerably from year to year,"[3] but in reality it appears to be the populations of other rodents that fluctuate greatly, and in doing so affect the numbers of dormice using boxes.

The sort of fluctuations suggested in the dormouse populations just do not tally with an animal that is said to produce relatively few young each year. In some sites wood mice can make nest boxes almost totally dormouse free zones. It appears that each year 10 per cent of sites with nest boxes often record no dormice. I have suffered enough "empty" boxes over the years, and have seen far too many wood mice. It is depressing to read reports from sites, especially those with large numbers of boxes, where they often see no dormice and are pleased when eventually they see just one. For example, a site in Cumbria reported no dormice in 1997, but in 1998 reported just one and "plenty of wood mice."[4] Just think of all that misplaced effort and expense. It seems that dormice are thought to be so rare that the kudos of being able to say that dormice occur in a particular site is worth an enormous amount of effort. Placing hundreds of nest boxes in woodland would generally appear a waste of resources and people's time. For example, there were 500 boxes in Ribbesford Wood in 2006, and in October only twenty-three dormice were found.[5] To me this indicates that for some reason the dormice were not finding the boxes attractive, whereas this wood was held as good, as it was among the only twenty-one sites that recorded more than twenty dormice that October.

Wood mouse in a dormouse nest box. They are aggressive competitors, even killing dormice. They often take over dormouse nests in boxes

The National Dormouse Monitoring Programme does not seem to recognise the importance of the presence of other rodents in nest box studies. Most work has been carried out in hazel coppice woodlands. Such woods are mostly on calcareous soils in southern England, and these tend to be well drained, so that wood mice tend not to monopolise nest boxes to the degree that they do where the soils are wetter clays, although yellow-necked mice may be present. The predilection of wood mice for boxes in wetter habitats could partly explain why dormice populations are thought to be smaller in the north and west of Britain. Other factors that can influence dormouse use of boxes are numerous. They include use of the boxes by birds for both nesting and roosting, the presence of predators, such as weasels, the weather, the availability of natural nest sites and nesting material, the dormouse's previous experience of boxes, as well as the position and condition of the boxes.

In the National Dormouse Monitoring Programme boxes are supposed to be spaced in a regular grid with the boxes 20m apart, and to be checked monthly between the 15th and 25th of each month. Not surprisingly recent work on the Continent has shown that the spacing of boxes within a grid can give very different estimates of populations, as the greater the number of boxes per hectare the greater the abundance of adult dormice recorded. The population in some forests had been calculated at times to be as low as two or even less than one per hectare, when the boxes were put up at a density of four per hectare. Subsequent work has shown that if twice as many boxes were used, populations of up to sixteen adults per hectare were found.

The frequency of checking boxes can radically alter the number of dormice being recorded. Calculations have generally been based on monthly checks. However, work on the Continent using edible dormice, which were tagged using transponders so that they could be checked in the boxes without disturbance, showed that all the animals were found again only with daily checks; with less frequent checking up to 50 per cent of the animals would have been missed[6]. It is only because I have checked boxes in coastal scrub more frequently in the autumn that I have realised the good numbers of dormice in the area.

Young tits in a dormouse nest box. Competition with birds is an important factor in dormouse use of boxes

Living with Dormice

The weather can affect dormouse usage of boxes and can change so much within the ten-day window when the monthly checks are made, that even if everything else is equal, it could render results not comparable. Dormice seem to avoid boxes in hot weather and, depending on wood mouse activity, at times use them more in colder wet conditions. The condition of the boxes is also important. It is suggested that nest boxes made from outdoor plywood may survive for a decade or more. If these are left out year after year, more and more other animals will visit them, leaving their scent, which will deter dormice. Also, the boxes will deteriorate and become less waterproof, and therefore less attractive to dormice. It is not surprising that dormouse numbers are decreasing at some sites because, probably, so too is the condition of the boxes.

One feature that should be considered of great significance, is the skewed distribution of numbers of dormice found in boxes, as given in the results shown in issues of *The Dormouse Monitor*. The graphs given in these newsletters show that by far the majority of sites record ten or less animals per fifty boxes, a few sites have between ten and twenty per fifty boxes, but a significant group in some years have twenty-five or more, with some so large that they are omitted from the graphs. In the 2004 results twenty of the 167 sites reported did not record any dormice, or evidence of dormice using any of the boxes. However, of greater significance are the seven results with over twenty dormice per fifty boxes. Four of these had forty or more and the highest had sixty-five dormice per fifty boxes. Such high numbers have been called "extraordinary" but occur often enough to be thought significant, and should not be left off the graphs because they do not fit on! Such "extremely high" results show us more of the true nature of dormouse populations than the normally low results. Very high numbers of dormice using boxes are most probably due to a temporary absence of other rodents. The number of dormice that I have recorded at my main "monitoring" site is usually similar to the low numbers recorded in the National Dormouse Monitoring Programme; only rarely have I recorded mega numbers, and this was when wood mouse numbers appeared to have crashed. The mega numbers give some indication of real dormouse populations, but boxes would need to be put up in much greater numbers to indicate anything like true populations of dormice.

In terms of effort, time and money, dormice are now said to be one of the best-monitored British mammals but unfortunately most of the effort has been misplaced, as it is not known what is being measured. So although it is said that we have a good idea on how dormice are doing nationally, in fact this is not known, nor are the population densities in which they normally live. The dormouse seems to have been leading us all a merry dance, and is actually thriving and widespread, but as ever it remains very, very elusive.

Toad in a dormouse box. If boxes are ever attached to sloping trunks, toads will climb up and get into boxes — where they are then trapped. Boxes should always be attached to upright supports

Brown long-eared bat in a nest box. Bats will use dormouse boxes — but more frequently it seems that dormice will use bat boxes

Previous studies on dormice in Britain

Breeding potential of dormice

One of the weak links in the ecology of the dormouse is said to be its "low potential reproductive rate."[1] The commonest family size is given as four and it has been concluded "that dormice can usually rear only one successful litter a year" leading to an annual recruitment of perhaps only one to two per female, even in a good year.[2] Such a low reproductive rate would certainly cause problems to a small rodent. Added to which it is suggested: "Even in good breeding years most litters are not born until the end of July or the beginning of August."[2] In some exceptional years it has been said that dormice may produce young as early as June, but food resources would be scarce in midsummer and litters born early might suffer high mortality as a result.[3] In captivity dormice can produce more than one litter, but if dormice did produce second litters in the wild, it has been concluded, they would probably not be born in time to fatten up before the winter, and those failing to reach about 12-15 grams before hibernating are thought unlikely to survive.

It is true that the dormouse produces far fewer broods of young a year than other small rodents, but even so, its breeding potential appears to have been grossly underestimated. Such a breeding rate is far too low for a small rodent to survive: much larger populations and breeding rates are essential. On the Continent two peaks of breeding are usually reported, and three broods are occasionally found.[4] Two or three broods are certainly also possible in British summers, and I have found that litters of eight or even nine are not exceptional, and dormice not infrequently breed in their first year. Previous conclusions about British dormice again appear to be due to reliance on data from nest boxes. I have found that most, and on some sites all dormice seem to avoid using boxes for breeding in, and where they do, it is generally the younger, more inexperienced ones who tend to breed later and have smaller broods of young. Suggesting dormice do not breed until late summer because of food shortages does not allow for the fact that dormice rely on a much more insect based diet, and one that is at a maximum earlier in the year. With the idea that ripe fruit is needed for feeding young, but also for fattening up for hibernation (weight being said to be put on gradually during the autumn) the dormouse would indeed be left in a pickle!

Biologists too often study species in isolation, whereas a species is only a small part of a very intricate web of relationships. This indeed seems to have happened with previous studies on dormice and have led to the conclusion that dormice have few predators and are relatively safe when up in the branches. Such ideas are far too simplistic for the real world. Even though dormice can survive for up to five years in the wild, it is doubtful that they often do: the dormouse is just another rodent, as much food for predators as any other species of mouse, and it is killed by other, more numerous rodents with which it shares its habitat. Dormice therefore need a much higher productivity rate than suggested to survive.

The young are born naked with their eyes closed. These are several days old

Food

The habitat needed by the dormouse is said to be very exacting, as it has been concluded that it is a specialist feeder. "Anatomical evidence suggests that the dormouse is a specialist feeder. Radio-tracking and direct observation confirm this, revealing highly selective, arboreal feeding behaviour. Dormice choose flowers and fruits from a series of trees as each becomes seasonally available."[1] Thus it is stated that a high diversity of suitable shrubs and trees are needed, and the dormouse is critically dependent upon the quality, dispersion and timing of its food resources.[2] Such a supply of food as suggested here just does not occur in many habitats where the dormouse is actually found, and certainly not within the relatively small home area used by dormice, which are said not to venture much further than 100m from their nest sites.

Hawthorn bush in fruit. Dormice will open the pips in the haws to get at the kernels. The way they open them is just as diagnostic as the way they open hazel nuts

A consequence of thinking that the dormouse is reliant on seasonal flowers and fruits has been the conclusion: "A major problem for dormice is the period between the end of the main tree flower season and the beginning of the fruiting period" a gap that apparently can under certain circumstances last from mid-June until mid-August.[3] Even though it is said that, "At times of food scarcity dormice appear to supplement their diet with aphids and caterpillars – often taken from foliage high in oak trees,"[4] it is still maintained that July is difficult, because flowers are over and fruits not yet ripe. Although insects are listed as high-grade foods taken by dormice, they do not seem to be accepted as the important food that they must be. Dormice are voracious feeders on insects: July is a peak season for insects and a peak season for dormouse breeding. Dormice live in so many habitats where there are few flowers – among conifers, in salt-blasted coastal scrub, or hedgerows composed of few species or that are cut each year so there are few flowers or fruits – that they must be feeding largely on some other type of food, and their predilection for insects certainly points to these being a major source.

It has been claimed that hazel nuts are "Almost essential and a principal source of food before hibernation."[5] However, hazel nuts have often all gone before dormice have finished rearing their young in the autumn, and they must often rely on insect food for putting on weight before hibernation. Hazel not only produces nuts; it has been found to be one of the dormouse's favourite trees in June, a time when faecal analysis shows that insects can account for up to 80 per cent of its diet.[6] The importance of insects has been grossly underestimated.

Dormice thrive in many habitats in which they cannot rely on a sequence of flowers and fruits. They appear to be very versatile omnivores able to adapt their diets to their surroundings. A reliance on sequential food is a common strategy in the tropics, but is rare and very risky in a temperate and unpredictable climate. Very few British ancient woods have a mix of species to produce anything like the food succession that dormice are said to require, and certainly not within the confines of supposed dormouse territory. In the tropics animals relying on such a strategy have to move long distances to find their food, and do not keep to small territories, as do dormice.

Weight increase before hibernation has been described as a gradual process and it has been said that young dormice "need to weigh at least 12-15 grams before hibernation in order to be fat enough to survive the winter."[?] The idea that dormice could get through hibernation at such weights takes no account of the sudden weight increases that young dormice achieve in the last two weeks before hibernation: 15 grams is merely the size they need to be before they can put on extra weight. The normal hibernation weight is at least 28 grams, well above adult summer weight.[7]

Previous studies on dormice in Britain

Habitat

As the dormouse is believed to be a specialist feeder, it is not surprising that it is thought to occur only in limited habitats that can provide for its special needs. Initially it was said to have a "strict dependence on woodland."[1] And based on the presumption of its selective feeding, it was said that it "needs habitat containing a lot of different types of shrubs and trees in order to ensure a continuous supply of food through the changing seasons."[2] It was suggested that suitable woodland is rarely found except in ancient deciduous woods where there is likely to be a heterogeneous mix of enough species to provide dormice with the required sequence of flowers and fruits. Ancient woodlands are areas where it is believed that there has been woodland, even if only in the form of plantations, since at least 1600AD. The best habitats are given as "mixed communities of hazel with some mature oak and an array of soft-mast-producing shrubs."[3] And if this was not enough, it is said that, even where there is a suitable botanical diversity, the wood must also have an appropriate physical structure, as dormice need a good continuous understorey of shrubs with well spaced standard trees, so that the understorey is not shaded, and the shrubs produce a good crop of flowers and fruits. Without this suitable woodland structure, it is said, dormice do not thrive! It is also suggested that much ancient woodland has become unsuitable for dormice owing to lack of management, especially coppicing, and interventionist conservation management is required to maintain the right type of habitat and hence the continued survival of the dormouse.[3]

Woods have previously been thought to be essential for dormice. But in reality dormice can also be found in almost any type of hedge or scrub

More recently it has been acknowledged that dormice "are also found in other woodland habitats including areas dominated by oak and holly, birch or oak/ash woodlands."[4] But it is still maintained that their principal habitat is the shrub layer of mixed deciduous woodland, and the occurrence of dormice in other "unusual" places should not deflect from the importance of the ancient woodlands, as other woods "are almost certainly poor habitats for dormice."[5]

Where woodland becomes mature with no secondary layer and there is no surrounding hedgerow, it is suggested that the wood cannot provide the necessary cover or food sources for dormice. Dormice are even said to have become locally extinct in woods that have matured and developed a closed canopy. The evidence from dormice not using boxes put up for several years has been said to prove their extinction. In one wood, dormice were deemed extinct as they had ignored boxes in place for three years "despite the fact that boxes were soon found and used" by yellow-necked mice.[3] What better reason could there be for the dormice to steer clear of the boxes!

It has been said that dormice can persist at the edge of their geographic range at locations where overall tree and shrub diversity is particularly high as such habitats are more likely to provide a continuous source of food. However, some of the most northerly known sites for dormice have been in such habitats as areas of conifers and of gorse, which are species poor.

All the evidence that I have been able to find indicates that not only are dormice found in all types and structures of woodland, they are also widespread in nearly every type of arboreal habitat, even in patches of scrub or brambles. Hazel coppice is rarely found except in ancient woodland and is the easiest habitat in which to find evidence of dormice, and in which to study dormice with nest boxes, though they appear to be equally abundant in most other arboreal habitats.

Living with Dormice

Dormouse presence in conifer plantations

Conifers are still held to be among the more "unusual" places where dormice are beginning to turn up. It has been suggested that extensive plantation forestry is unlikely to support significant numbers of dormice, as the reduced species diversity would not provide a sequence of arboreal foods: "Dormice are sometimes found associated with conifers, especially where these have been planted among hazel and other deciduous species. Conifers shade out other important shrubs, yet dormice sometimes seem to remain. … However, they are unlikely to thrive in purely coniferous woodland."[1] There seems to be no reason why dormice should not survive equally as well, if not better, in conifers, as they do in some areas of salt-blasted scrub or managed hedges. Present day evidence indicates that dormice can thrive in pure conifer plantations.

Dormouse presence in hedges

Initially it was concluded that dormice are dependent on woodland, but more recently it has been acknowledged that they are to be found in hedges: "Hedges can be like long strips of ideal dormouse habitat and the animals may actually live there permanently. At other times they may simply use hedges as a sheltered dispersal route, enabling them to cross otherwise open ground between small patches of woodland."[1] But provisos are added and it is suggested that the best hedges that dormice actually live in are large ancient ones "near to woods and with plenty of different shrubs within." It is even suggested that dormice, because of their perceived need for species-rich habitats, are indicators of ancient hedgerows. Such observations came chiefly from some recent surveys, which concluded that there has been a catastrophic decline of dormice in hedgerows: "There has been a 64 per cent decline of dormouse occurrence in hedgerows since the late 1970s, equating to a red alert decline of 70 per cent over twenty-five years. The long, historic decline of the dormouse is thus continuing at a rapid rate."[2]

The main survey method used to determine the presence of dormice in hedges was nest tubes. Nesting tubes, although generally more attractive than boxes to dormice in hedgerows because they are less attractive to wood mice, are in no way the perfect panacea for such work. It is difficult to find suitable places to anchor tubes in hedges in positions where dormice are actually likely to use them: it is easiest in large unkempt hedges and often impossible in frequently

bottom left: A dormouse nest being pointed out in a low salt-sculpted hedge near the sea

bottom right: Close up of the nest

Previous studies on dormice in Britain

flailed hedges. The quality of the undergrowth associated with a hedge seems to determine wood mouse activity, which in turn seems to determine dormouse use of tubes. Large unkempt hedges usually shade out undergrowth, whereas in frequently cut hedges more undergrowth develops, and the associated populations of wood mice may be greater. Tubes need checking regularly if proof of dormouse presence is to be found, as wood mice regularly take over dormouse nests built in tubes, in preference to having to build their own from scratch. In the studies concluding that dormice are rare in hedgerows, the tubes were often put up in spring and not rechecked until the dormice had gone into hibernation, leaving wood mice more than enough time to trash any dormouse nests. The suggestion that some dormice "settle in the hedgerows and live their whole lives safely concealed among the interlocking branches"[3] totally ignores the constant rivalry between different rodents living in hedges, let alone the presence of predators.

After the grass verge had been cut along this road, a dormouse nest was found down in a clump of grass at the base of the fence

Dispersal of dormice: sink or source populations?

Fragmentation of woodland is said to disrupt populations, as dormice are said not to travel very far and to be reluctant to cross open ground. It has even been suggested "fragmentation is probably the key reason for the decline of the dormouse."[1] The resultant smaller populations are deemed to be liable to suffer local extinctions, and not be able to recolonise sites from which they have been lost. The idea that dormice are poor dispersers seems to be based on rather few observations made while radio tracking dormice: "The short distances travelled by dormice … their small body size and strong arboreality, all have profound implications for the dispersal potential of the species. The continuous arboreal activity we recorded seems to preclude dispersal over open ground between woods."[2] This, together with the erroneous idea that dormice are specialist feeders needing specialist habitats, has led to the dormouse being considered an ideal model species for the study of the effects of habitat fragmentation in a species confined to a particular habitat.[3]

It has been said that dormice can live permanently in some hedges, but "hedges are also important dispersal routes, a vital lifeline linking dormouse populations in small copses."[4] To avoid local extinctions it is suggested new hedgerow linkages should be put in place, and where new roads are constructed, bridges covered by arboreal habitat are advocated. Indeed, one such bridge has already been built in Kent.[5] Even woodland rides and woodland clearings are said to be serious impediments to dormice moving around, and to their being able to exploit even local resources.[2] It is suggested that branches should be tied together across rides, and rope bridges put across wider gaps. Experiments have even been carried out that claim to show that gaps in hedges constrain movement of dormice along them.[6] The dormice were only tracked for a single night in their new surroundings, and some dormice had crossed the smaller gaps of one metre, where they would have had to have gone down to ground level. In the bewilderment of a first

Living with Dormice

night in a strange area, a dormouse should not be expected to move far, in the same way as a dormouse when first put in a cage does not explore much during its first night and just grabs the first food that it knows.

General acceptance of the idea that dormice are strict arborealists has led to such comments as, "Short distances, possibly as little as 100m, form absolute barriers to dispersal, unless arboreal routes are available."[7] The concept that dormice will not move around without arboreal connections is misconceived; they are often found in patches of scrub without arboreal connections to other areas. Fragmentation of woodland is unlikely to cause any major problems to their survival, and clearance of arboreal habitat would have to be on a very widespread scale to cause extinction of dormice in any area. Destruction of habitat has doubtless affected the dormouse in some areas, and this will have happened especially in arable regions. However, over much of the countryside, especially in areas where the farming is predominantly pastoral, there does not appear to have been radical enough change to eradicate the dormouse. It is still grossly under recorded.

In maintaining that extensive ancient woodland is the core habitat for dormice, it is suggested that others habitats may be ephemeral, and the occurrence of dormice in these "non-typical" habitats may merely indicate the presence of a thriving population in adjacent woodland.[4] It has also been suggested that in some areas, such as Herefordshire, at least 20ha of isolated woodland is required to support a self-sustaining dormouse population in the long term, but where sites are well connected by large hedges to other suitable sites, sites as small as 5ha can contain dormice.[8] Where woodland is more fragmented, such as in the Cotswolds, it has even been said that the viable area for a dormouse population is as much as 50ha.[9] Smaller areas are held to support only sink populations rather than source populations. A source population is defined as a net exporter of individuals, whereas a sink population is dependent on the import of individuals from a larger area.

Dormice are actually so widespread in hedgerows and scrub, well away from any woodland, that in no way can they be thought of as dependent on large areas of woodland, but rather as denizens of most arboreal habitat. Dormice live in much higher densities, and populations are viable in much smaller habitats than previously suggested. Instead of thinking of sink populations in terms of woods under 20ha, thinking in terms of bramble patches would be more realistic!

A meadow just inland of Chesil Bank. Here dormouse nests have been found in the hedge and in isolated clumps of scrub

Problems with the British climate

It is believed that "the ecology of the dormouse forms a long chain of weak links. If any of them break, local extinction is likely."[1] And it has been concluded that the unpredictable climate of Britain is such that a run of "bad" years could cause local populations of dormice to become extinct, because of their low population density and low potential reproductive rate.[1,2] Then it is concluded that extinctions are likely to be permanent as the dormouse is ill equipped to reinvade because it uses only small patches of specialised habitats and travels only short distances.

As well as being susceptible to a succession of "bad" years, it is thought that dormice "are better suited to a continental climate of warm dry summers and cold dry winters and they are, therefore, likely to be sensitive to climate change."[3] In Britain it is suggested that global warming and consequent warmer winters will cause the dormice problems: "If a hibernator is warmed, its fat reserves are depleted faster by a raised metabolic rate and may be exhausted before the end of winter."[1] As well as problems with hibernation it is suggested that as the dormouse is such a specialised animal, it is very sensitive to the effects of weather on the timing and abundance of food. Hence it is stated that global warming could push dormice to the brink of extinction in the north of England, not only because of the milder winters but also because of warmer summers. The warmer summer weather is said to cause fruit to ripen earlier, so that food supply would end earlier and the dormouse would be forced into hibernation earlier, making its winters longer.

It is even suggested that the limited period during which hazel nuts are available may be affected by the weather and may be critical for dormice as they are held to be essential for dormice when fattening up before hibernation.

The dormouse is at the edge of its range in Britain, and it is most probably climatic factors that limit its distribution. However, progressive local extinctions owing to a run of "bad" years are unlikely to occur in the way suggested. Dormice do not live in isolated patches of specialised habitat, and are mobile and capable of reinvading any local areas. Many of the areas from which dormice are thought to have disappeared over the past hundred years, have not been searched thoroughly enough, and with increased interest in dormice, they are gradually being relocated. This is, of course, a slow process because the dormouse is very elusive!

Rather than having so many weak links in its biology, the dormouse appears to be a very adaptable animal. As well as living in parts of the Continent that have very long, hard winters, it occurs over much of southern Europe and even in areas such as Sicily, which have a Mediterranean climate and where it does not always hibernate in winter. So warmer winters should not be too problematic. It would seem that warmer winters could be less physiologically stressful than some of the Continental winters, when dormice hibernate for up to seven months and may at times have to endure temperatures well below freezing for five months. The dormice in the coastal regions of Dorset have coped with warm winters for many years, and some found in late winter have still been above normal summer weights. Hazel nuts are in no way essential for fattening up, and run out long before most dormice go into hibernation. They probably rely mostly on insects just before hibernation and warmer weather increases the insect supply.

In wet habitats there is often too much competition for a dormouse to get a look in a box. Here there were 62 garden snails and three wood mice — the latter were too shy to stay for photos

dormice can exist in a Mediterranean climate where they do not always hibernate in winter

Conservation action for dormice

The dormouse is held to be a rare animal. Because of this perceived rarity it is not only a protected species, but also has been made a priority species with an individual Species Action Plan in the UK Biodiversity Action Plan. It is said that the research carried out has revealed reasons for the decline of the dormouse,[1,2] and established a sound scientific basis for the Species Recovery Programme for the dormouse.[3]

Three main approaches are advocated in the programme to help dormice. Firstly, to defend them where they are still found by means of habitat management, particularly reinstating coppicing and removal of excess standard trees in woods. In addition putting up nest boxes is advocated, as it is said to aid dormice and allow monitoring. Secondly, by arranging reintroductions, using captive bred animals, into counties predominantly in the Midlands and northern England where they are thought to have become locally extinct or extremely rare over the last century, associated with the creation of arboreal links to adjacent habitats to help dormice spread. Finally, to raise the profile and the plight of the dormouse with the general public by means of Nut Hunts, dormouse training days, and other publicity. It is reported that numbers of dormice are still declining nationally, but that there are grounds for optimism as the rate of decrease is slowing. This decrease is thought to show that conservation efforts are beginning to work and that dormice should be able once again to thrive in our hedges and woods.

It actually appears that there is not a dramatic decline in dormouse numbers, nor do they need the assistance suggested, as they have been in our woods and hedges all the time. The idea that they have declined so drastically is based on lack of records (well, the dormouse is elusive!), on results derived from nest box data, and on the Nut Hunts. The low population density and low reproduction rates that have been given for dormice again appear to be based on misinterpretation of data from nest boxes. Nest boxes cannot always prove the presence of dormice, let alone indicate the state of a dormouse population.

The dormouse is a much more widespread and abundant animal than is generally realised, and most of the supposed threats to its existence are without foundation. It is said that one of the factors producing the decline is the "fragmentation, deterioration and loss of specialised habitat" and the specialised habitat is generally only to be found in ancient woodland.[2] Loss of ancient woodland is a disaster for wildlife in general, especially for species dependent on woodland habitat. Dormice do well in this habitat but are not dependent on it, as they thrive in most arboreal habitats. So loss of such habitat *per se* would not be crucial to their survival in any area. The supposed threat of the deterioration of dormouse habitat is apparently due to the decline in coppicing in the woodlands, and as this is said to be highly beneficial to dormice, it is suggested that this needs to be reinstated to provide the specialised habitat that they require. In fact, coppicing does not seem to help dormice, except perhaps to make them use nest boxes more readily because of the removal of natural nesting sites. It does, however, remove much insect rich habitat, which would be more beneficial to them. So long as arboreal habitats in general are conserved, the dormouse will happily carry on doing its own thing. Fortunately, few, if any, of the perceived problems apply to the real world of the dormouse, but its real problems of competition and predators have been virtually ignored.

Management of habitat: to coppice or not to coppice

It was suggested in the early part of the last century that the reduction in coppicing was possibly an important factor in dormice becoming scarcer.[1] This conclusion still holds sway: "Perhaps the greatest single cause of Dormouse decline results from a subtle form of habitat loss due to reduction in woodland management, particularly coppice management."[2] It has even been suggested that in Wales, "Coppicing is now so infrequent that its lack is probably the main current constraint on distribution in all counties."[3]

Restoration of coppice is advocated as the main means of salvation for the dormouse, as hazel coppicing became "uneconomic in the twentieth century resulting in many woodlands becoming sub-optimal habitats for dormice."[4] The coppicing regime recommended for dormice is one of a long cycle of fifteen to twenty years to allow hazel to fruit well.

Coppicing used to be a common method of exploiting woodlands, usually with short-term rotations to obtain small-sized wood for such jobs as hurdle-making. When coppicing for dormice, a long-term rotation is said to be essential as the hazel produces few nuts before about seven or eight years, and coppicing should be carried out in a mosaic pattern, not in adjacent blocks as it would have been in commercial cropping. It would seem that the earlier intensive management of woodland, said to have been the factor that kept dormice common, was more likely to have been relatively harmful. Woods coppiced today for such tasks as hurdle making are certainly not dormouse friendly.

The dormouse has been made such a high profile species that management with dormice in mind is having a huge influence on the way woods are managed. Not only does management based on the requirements of single species often have unfortunate ecological consequences for the habitat as a whole, but the management advocated for dormice is more likely to be destroying good dormouse habitat than producing any benefits for them. It has been said that coppicing to produce bushes that provide a good crop of flowers and fruit is essential for dormice. It is salutary that in Dorset, dormice are often found in areas of overgrown hazel

Coppicing hazel for hurdle making. Most coppicing in the past would have been too frequent to have been dormouse friendly

coppice, where there is little, if any production of nuts. In Cumbria, in some of the most northerly sites known in Britain, dormice similarly occur in derelict coppice, which is very poor in terms of variety and quantity of plant food sources. In view of the dormouse's greater reliance on insects rather than hazel nuts, coppicing does not seem justified in the name of dormouse conservation. It is ironic that the very management that is advocated for dormice in woodland is probably, at least temporarily, removing the very conditions that suit dormice best. The total production of insect food in dense overgrown coppice or in areas of high forest is far greater than in recent coppice. Coppiced areas may appear dormouse friendly because it is here that they tend more readily to use nest boxes because natural nesting sites are in shorter supply. One of the reasons given for the presumed extinction of dormice in the northern counties of England is that coppicing stopped there earlier than in the south.[2] Coppicing does not help dormice, and dormice are found in the north in such habitats as areas of gorse, in the same way that they are in the south.

Older hazel coppice is better habitat for dormice, as there will be a greater volume of habitat with larger insect populations

Re-instatement of coppicing is now occurring chiefly in the name of conservation, and is seemingly an icon of present day ecology. It is often carried out as the panacea for all woodland management. Ecological management unfortunately often believes that traditional management should be reinstated, whereas traditional management was developed purely to exploit wildlife and may not be the best way forward for wildlife today.[5] When advocating coppicing for conservation, there should be a clear idea of the intended benefits. Coppicing not only may be detrimental to dormouse habitat, but if not carried out carefully can turn woodland into glorified scrub, when there are many rare species reliant on mature woodland. That is not to say that coppicing should not be carried out, as there are species that depend on open habitat within woodlands. Conversely there is a range of organisms that depend on neglected hazel coppice, which presents a more structurally diverse habitat with more ecological niches. Species that are generally associated with mature woodland habitat are likely to be sensitive to woodland management, and to be less easily conserved than species that can live within commoner habitat, such as scrub. Dormice come within the latter category, as they seem to be denizens of most types of arboreal habitats. Any woodland management should not unduly affect the survival of dormice, so long as the management is not too drastic and is not over too large an area. Coppicing may be useful in increasing the numbers of early flowering woodland herbs, but may do so at the expense of invertebrate diversity, through decreased structural diversity of the environment. It would therefore seem advisable always to have a mosaic of woodland blocks leaving some of them unmanaged.

High forest, with little understorey, has been mistakenly dismissed as of little use to dormice. Part of the woodland management that is advocated for them is the removal of "excess" standard trees, so that too much shade is not cast on the understorey, thus promoting abundant flowering and fruiting of the shrubs.[6] It is even suggested that where there are large canopy trees such as mature oaks, they should not exceed more than about 10 per hectare, so that canopy trees cover only 25-30 per cent of the area. Thinning of young trees so that they do not become spindly with few horizontal branches would seem justified, as dormice do seem to prefer a dense leafy habitat with plenty of horizontal pathways. But the removal of large canopy trees for the sake of dormice is ecological sacrilege; it is removing habitat, not only good for dormice but needed by many rare species reliant on mature woodland. Such management together with coppicing can turn whole areas of woodland into scrub, associated with rank

Three young dormice in torpor in the Spring. Having been disturbed, two of them are determined to hide their eyes from the sun — the third being more sleepy is overturned by the others

Dormouse waking up from summer torpor, squinting in the bright sunlight

weedy species rather than woodland flowers. It is an example of misplaced management in the name of a single species, rather than considering an ecological community in its entirety: woods need trees!

It is an unfortunate side effect of the dormouse being such a high profile species that many reserve managers seem to think they have failed if they do not see dormice in the boxes that they have put up for them. Rather than trying to understand why the dormice are not using the boxes, they are likely to try the drastic "conservation" management that is advocated for dormice. One report stated that "dormice records this year are still negative" and that " considerable debate occurred over the felling of large canopy trees, which is in line with the policy of opening up the woods for a better understorey for wild flowers and particularly for dormice."[7] Woodland managers have to be aware of wildlife in its fullest sense, and be less swayed by their fondness for charismatic species such as the dormouse. Fortunately, it does seem that many of them are reluctant to thin canopy trees for the sake of dormice.

Removal of old mature trees in the name of dormice makes one shudder. Removing old trees is abhorrent management for conservation. It is removing a whole large multi-dimensional ecosystem, about which we know very little as yet. Even old shrub species, such as hawthorn, can have a different epiphytic flora and different insects living at their tops. We decry the removal of tropical rainforests, but we have yet to understand what we are losing ourselves. "We expose ourselves to accusations of hypocrisy from other countries if we encourage them to protect their forests, while recommending that we continue to chop down our own by traditional methods."[5] I have seen too many parts of woods ruined by "conservationists". In one wood the removal of large, old oaks, home for rare lichens, together with coppicing, has left rather rank grassland with well-spaced coppiced hazel. In another wood, where grazing by deer had not been controlled, coppicing led to weedy wasteland dominated by thistles. Both such habitats could have been reproduced from farmland, without despoiling ancient woodland.

Managing conifers

Dormice often occur and seem to thrive in conifer plantations; it is dubious if any particular habitat management is necessary for them. In the belief that dormice are rare and declining, research has been undertaken to help provide woodland managers with advice on how to carry out operations, particularly where ancient woodland sites have been planted with conifers.[1] It is suggested that thinning conifer stands in such woods should not be delayed, as dormice populations could be critically affected by the thickening of the conifer canopy and consequent decline of the shrub layer. This is doubtful, as dormice seem very at home in dense conifers, in the shelter of which there may be larger densities of insects, and where there is no ground flora there may even be the advantage of less competition from wood mice.

Some of the ideas on thinning conifers will be good for wildlife in general, but do not seem at all necessary for the survival of dormice. Avoiding large clear fells is certainly vital, but maintaining or creating connections within the wood, to the degree suggested, can in no way be essential. Reconstruction of low level connections across rows using brash or even resorting to pushing trees over at an angle to create connecting bridges, is going unnecessarily far for an animal that is quite capable of running across roads and living in isolated clumps of bramble.

The lack of undergrowth in many conifer plantations may help dormice, as wood mice prefer areas with dense undergrowth

Providing nest boxes for dormice

The provision of nest boxes in woods has been suggested as a major conservation measure to help dormice, because it is believed that they provide them with dry safe nesting places. Unfortunately, nest boxes with a single entrance can act like traps: they attract predators such as weasels and competitors such as wood mice, and dormice often seem very wary of using them. By all means have a few boxes so that people can be shown dormice, as this can help enthuse people to become more involved with wildlife issues. But remember that on most sites it is the more aggressive and abundant wood mice that will really appreciate the boxes, and dormice are probably far safer placing their nests in natural sites. Wood mice nests have no real structure to them, so they have to be on the ground or in a structure such as a box. One can but hope that naturally placed dormouse nests in among vegetation are of little use to wood mice.

Putting up nest boxes for dormice often only provides nesting sites for wood mice

Bridges for dormice

Woodland fragmentation is one of the factors suggested as a reason for the demise of the dormouse. It is said that dormice do not like to come down to the ground, and splitting up populations could cause extinctions of the resultant smaller populations. Provisions of new hedgerows to provide linkages between woods, although in all probability unnecessary, would be good for wildlife in general and the management that has been suggested for hedges, with reduced cutting to promote greater production of fruit, would fortunately help not only dormice but most wildlife.

In several counties where road developments have bisected woodland, vegetated bridges and rope bridges have been installed to help re-link the dormouse habitats. This has entailed considerable expense, for which there can be little, if any justification. Dormice are territorial and only move limited distances, so for most of the year such bridges would be of assistance to only very few of them. It is doubtful if rope bridges would ever be considered safe runways by dormice, especially if used by other rodents. In some cases feeding stations have been placed near the end of bridges to attract dormice but they also attract wood mice, and hence probably do more harm than good. When young are dispersing in the autumn they can easily run across roads, which they are far more likely to do than use narrow bridges of any sort.

Dormice are often found in isolated patches of scrub, as above, so the provision of bridges is totally unnecessary

Reintroductions

Reintroduction of dormice into areas, where they are thought to have become extinct, or very rare over the last century, has been said to be one of the main tools underpinning the delivery of the Biodiversity Action Plan for the species. It is held to be one of the most effective conservation methods to help the dormouse. The need for reintroductions is explained thus: "Dormice have often been lost as a result of inappropriate woodland management in the past. The habitat may now be very suitable, but the strongly arboreal behaviour of dormice means that they are unlikely to return unaided, hence the need for reintroductions."[1]

Reintroductions have been carried out in eleven counties since 1993, mainly in the Midlands and northern England. The cost in time and money has been considerable, but it is held that the drastic decline called for desperate measures. The "reintroduction" schemes have elicited such responses as: "Reintroduction schemes can be difficult to get right and I am impressed the project has been so successful;" and, "Without projects like these the dormouse would face extinction."

Reintroduction schemes do not seem justified, as the true distribution and population densities of dormice have yet to be correctly ascertained. The dormouse appears to be so widespread and plentiful, at least in southern England, that it should not be considered a priority species for reintroduction. It is a very charismatic species, and it is such species that are most likely to be considered for reintroduction. Such reintroductions owe more to public relations than to conservation, and the money could be better spent. Reintroductions could even be dangerous, if disease is imported into an already established population. Only a relatively small genetic base is introduced with a reintroduction, as the number of animals used is often in the region of about fifty or less. Yet there have been worries about potential genetic deterioration in dormice where it is perceived that populations have become isolated by roads and such like, to the extent of incurring the expense of putting up some sort of bridge to reconnect the populations.

The reintroductions carried out seem to have been very successful. This may be partly due to the fact that captive bred dormice are already conditioned to using boxes. If a dormouse has previous experience of a box they may be more likely to use a box again. Such behaviour may explain the good results generally obtained in the first years of a reintroduction. Worries that some reintroductions are not doing as well in later years may merely be due to the deterioration of the boxes and the progressive use and tainting of the boxes by other rodents.

The woods chosen for reintroductions are not just any wood, but ones of 50ha or more that correspond to the assumed "prime" dormouse habitat with many species of trees, a thick undergrowth, and management that is producing lots of fruiting hazel. It is hardly conceivable in such large woods that the habitat could have deteriorated so much over the last hundred years that dormice would have become extinct. As they appear to thrive in high forest, the changes in management, such as cessation of coppicing, are not capable of producing extinction. Therefore, either the dormice are still there and just being their normal elusive selves, or there must be something very wrong with the wood. There seems little point in reintroducing dormice to such woods before they have been studied far more closely.

It can be a long and difficult task to prove the presence of dormice in some woods, and it is doubtful whether the pre-release checks for presence of dormice in the woods were as thorough as is necessary for this very elusive animal. A reintroduction was made in Warwickshire, only a few miles from a known site, and a subsequent survey found dormice to be present in six woods spread across the county.[2] Such a distribution would suggest that dormice could be fairly widespread in the county. It is hard to accept that they had become extinct in Yorkshire, another area of reintroductions.[3] The records for Yorkshire in the nineteenth century suggest a fairly widespread occurrence and there have been a number of records from the twentieth century.[4] The efficacy of the reintroduction carried out in 2006 to the Bradfield Woods, Suffolk, is questionable.[5] Dormice have been recorded in these woods but recent monitoring was said to have come up with negative results. Not only are dormice known from a series of other sites in that county, but it would take many years of monitoring in a large ancient wood before one should consider the possibility that dormice might have become extinct. Now more thorough searches are being made, the dormouse is progressively being refound in counties where it was once thought to be extinct.

The dormice collected for the breeding schemes have generally been juveniles thought to be born too late to fatten up sufficiently for hibernation. Juveniles weighing 15 grams or less in late October are considered to come into this category. This may be rather too soon in the autumn to write off these youngsters, and it shows no realisation of the rapid pre-hibernal weight gain that dormice undergo.

> the dormouse appears to be so **widespread** that it should not be considered a priority species for reintroduction

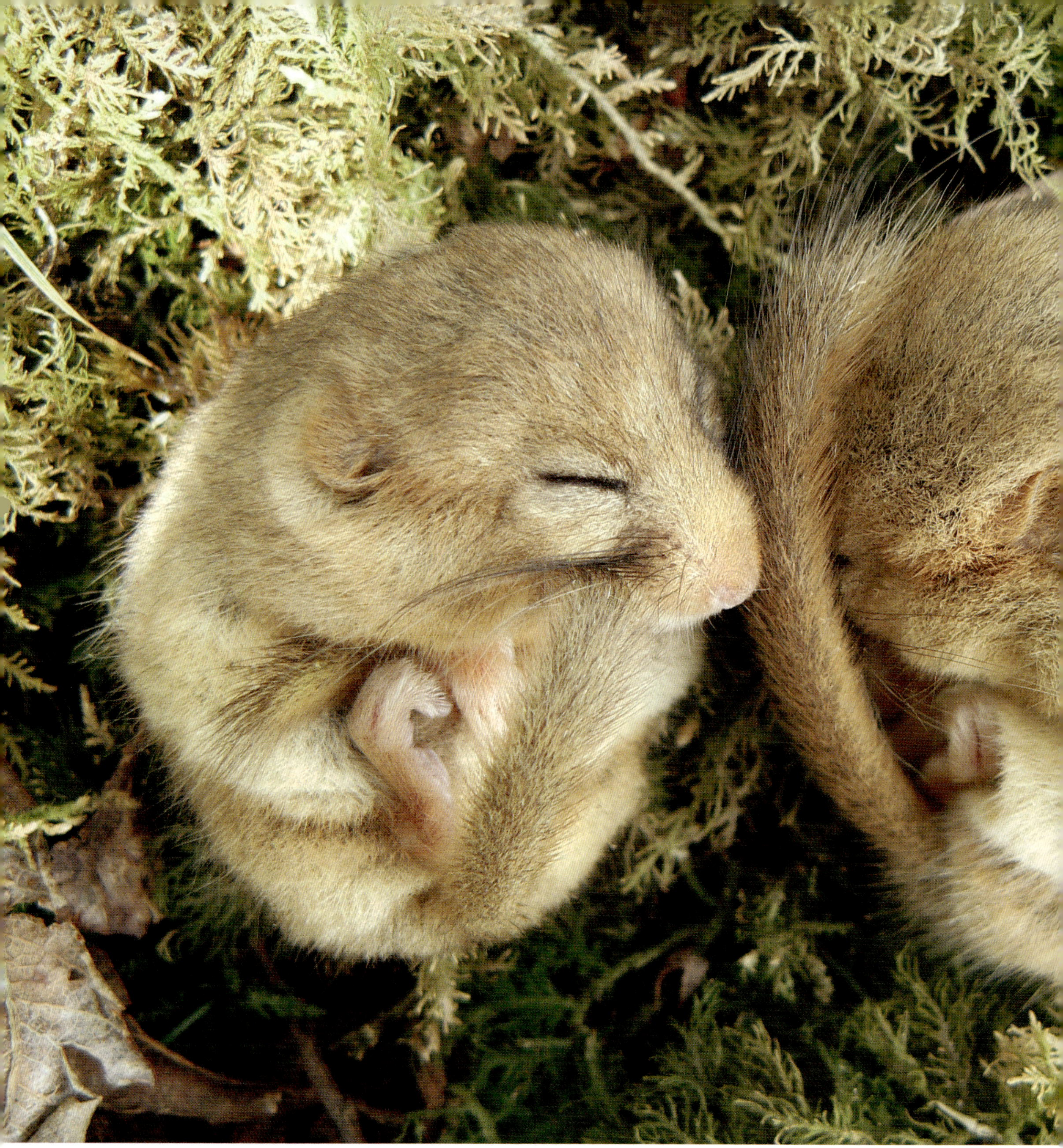

Conclusions

When I was working as a marine biologist, I was perturbed that I was expected to throw my data into a computer without having to understand the meaning of the data. During my literature searches on algae I came across this quote by Dr J.W.G. Lund, of the Fresh Water Biological Station, "A mathematical approach is very valuable but anyone who works with natural populations knows that we need more observational data. He also knows from experience that some mathematical and other attempts to explain the ecology of phytoplankton are of limited value – even erroneous – because of the need to make basic assumptions, which are not justified by the available data."

In science these days there is a cult of making measurements that can be submitted to statistical examination, and even ecology seems to be subservient to the straight and narrow path of planned experiments. But until we can understand dormice further, a more empirical approach, including observing dormice in the real world, is what is required. It would do no harm if at times we could go back to natural history observation as it was in Victorian times.

I agree that to guide the conservation and wildlife management policies for mammals, good data of their distribution and population trends are required. But even though the dormouse has been for such a long time one of the most thoroughly "monitored" mammals in Britain, I do not agree with the "official" findings. What is the good of statistics if one does not understand the data that one is subjecting to such analysis?

The approach to studying dormice and calculating populations has been too simplistic. Population sizes and trends have mostly been calculated using data from nest boxes. Dormice do not have a monopoly of nest boxes, and are indeed often in danger if they use them, but the competition with other mice and the presence of predators has been ignored.

The dormouse has been portrayed as a rare and declining animal. The ecology of the dormouse is said to contain a chain of weak links, with a low population density, low potential reproductive rate, having specialist food requirements seldom met except in ancient woodland and occasionally in large species rich hedgerows, and being vulnerable to changes and fragmentation of its arboreal habitat. The lack of coppicing has been seized upon as the prime reason for dormouse decline, and restoration of coppice advocated as the main means of salvation for the dormouse. If such problems and such solutions really were fact, it would be surprising that the dormouse survives in Britain at all. But these ideas have been repeatedly reproduced in literature. It is a good thing that dormice have not learnt to read books and just keep doing their own thing.

It was sheer chance that dormice were found in the coastal scrub in our garden, habitat that in no way fits that said to be needed by dormice. Years of working with impenetrable blackthorn scrub and brambles has had its thorny problems, but has shown me that dormice are widespread, tough, opportunistic omnivores. I have found that they are not specialist animals restricted to only certain arboreal habitats. They do not have exacting habitat requirements, and are exceptionally versatile and very resourceful animals. The evidence that I have obtained also indicates that they are in no way as rare as they are generally held to be, and indeed must surely, as in Dorset, be widespread in the more southern parts of their range in Britain. Doubtless they are not so common in the northern parts of their range, but are most probably still grossly under-recorded.

When more people start looking in habitats other than woodlands, the true distribution of dormice may become more apparent.

Patience and tenacity are needed when studying dormice; they are very elusive animals, and only when conditions are just right do they seem to show up in anything like their true abundance in any particular habitat. Inland in Dorset, it was ten years of checking boxes before there was a critical crash in wood mouse numbers, and the subsequent use of boxes by dormice gave a more realistic insight into their abundance. In the scrub and hedgerows by the coast, I had been searching for nests for a similar length of time, before I found an abundance of nests. But here it seemed that a larger number of wood mice than normal had resulted in the dormice placing more nests in extreme positions, so that they were more easily visible.

There is still much to find out about dormice. All the survey methods have their uses and all have their limitations, but by using these, much more could be found out about their general distribution and the habitats they use. Previous interpretation of nest box data has unfortunately erroneously concluded that dormice are very rare. They have consequently been made a high profile species and yes, this has led to site protection, which is a good thing. However, the management practices applied for dormice may not have been the best for dormice, or for organisms reliant on mature woodland. Management of woodland should not be based on a single species, but rather on the habitat as a whole. However cute and attractive the dormouse, the less glamorous species still need to be remembered. In plans for dormouse conservation, it never seems to be said that one should check for ancient woodland species of lichens before removing standard trees, or check the epiphytic bryophytes of overgrown hazel before coppicing: habitats containing rare lichens and bryophytes would be just the ones where dormice would find plenty of insects for food.

> a more empirical approach, including observing dormice in the real world, is what is required

Dormice are difficult animals to study because they are so elusive. But however common, the dormouse still remains just as fascinating and enigmatic as that rare phantom of the ancient wood. How can dormice manage to live alongside the seemingly much more aggressive and more numerous wood mice, in the same hedgerow? How can dormice fatten up so rapidly for hibernation, even after their main food sources seem finished? Is hibernating an efficient method of getting through winter, when being in torpor appears to make dormice so vulnerable to predators?

Over the years I have been gradually honing and changing my ideas on dormice. They still amaze and astonish me as to their versatility and unpredictability. I feel that I am still far from really understanding them and their elusive ways. I do not expect readers to instantly take on board all they have read here, in the same way that it took me years to get my head round the fact that dormice are not the animals I had been reading about in books. But please do not just follow blindly what you have been told or what you have read previously. Go out and think and observe for yourselves. And please look in all arboreal habitats, not just in large woods and not just where there is hazel. I hope that I may have inspired some of you to take up the challenge of finding out more about this fascinating animal, and that this publication, with your help, may bring the study of dormice out of its time warp and into the new millennium.

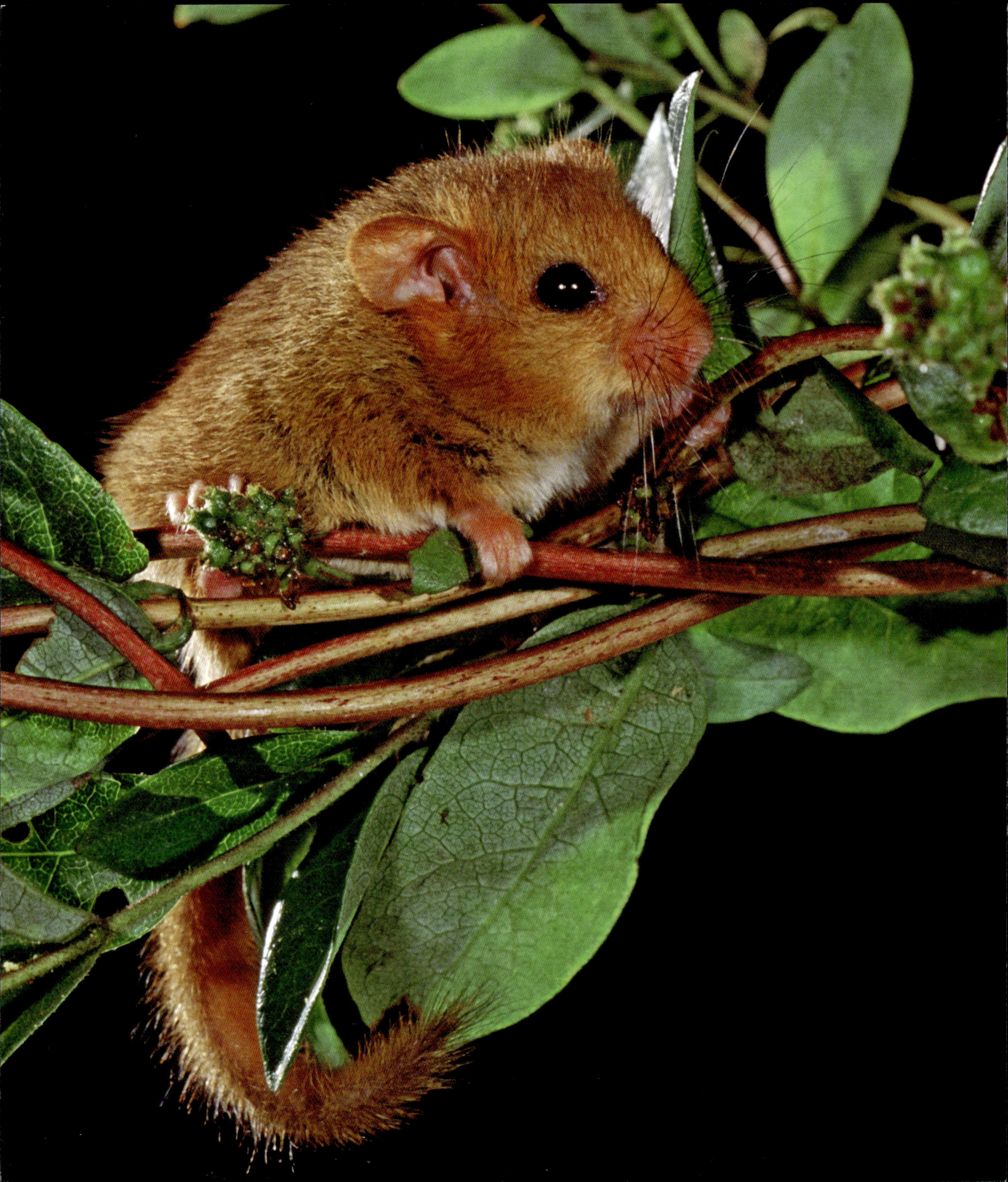

Appendix

My own experiences of monitoring dormice

This summary of the results from my nest boxes is an illustration of such work, though I concentrate mainly on the results that show how I have come to some of my conclusions about dormice. I especially wish to show why I think nest boxes are an inadequate source of data from which to deduce populations and breeding successes, and in some cases even the presence of dormice. Some of my results may be a useful comparison for the many other people who are checking nest boxes. At many sites very few dormice, if any, are seen each year. I hope that through my results people may realise why they are seeing so few dormice, and my conclusions may help them to assess some of the many factors that affect dormouse use of their own boxes.

I decided to try to study dormice in sites that previously would have been termed "unusual" or "odd" sites, but from my work I most certainly consider these sites to be perfectly normal dormouse habitat. Virtually all other nest box schemes are in woodland, and it did not seem worth duplicating these efforts. Working in coppiced hazel woodland would certainly have been easier. It would have saved many a scratch from wrestling with brambles and barbed wire, not to mention trying to push through face-high nettles. It would have saved tubes from being flailed into oblivion, and boxes being knocked to the ground by cattle using them as rubbing posts. I have often had to contend with rapid growth of vegetation, especially brambles, and to cut my way through to the boxes.

Roy made the first set of boxes and then our neighbour, Jim, kindly went into mass production. Most of our sites, not being woods, were too small to accommodate the fifty boxes at 20m intervals, as stipulated by the National Dormouse Monitoring Programme. Putting boxes in grids is just not feasible in dense blackthorn or along hedgerows. At the height of my box studies I had about 175 boxes to check spread over five sites, with some of the sites incorporating several types of habitat. As I have now found that dormice do not appear to need boxes, which are not the safe nesting sites that they are said to be, I have drastically cut back on box numbers. I have only fifty boxes at one site, very few boxes at the other sites, and I am now using a more experimental approach.

Nest box use by dormice often seems correlated with habitat type, but by working in a range of sites, I have found that nest box use is actually more controlled by the abundance of competitors. I have so far carried out only a few tentative experiments, but they are helping to show more of the complexity of the factors involved in dormouse use of nest boxes. Over the years I have just kept plodding on: some years the dormice did not seem to want to co-operate and use the boxes, but later I found even the negative results enlightening. As I find some answers to the dormouse conundrum, even more questions arise, but that is the way with any research project.

Kingcombe Meadows Reserve

I am very grateful to the Dorset Wildlife Trust for allowing me to work on two of their reserves. My main nest box scheme is on their Kingcombe Meadows Reserve in West Dorset. The reserve covers one of the largest areas of unimproved neutral grassland in southern England; it is some 177ha in size. The area is made up of many fields, surrounded by ancient hedgerows, and there are a few small copses. It has been called "the farm that time forgot" and its meadows and small fields represent a unique example of farmland of the past.

Much of the habitat at Kingcombe is similar, and can provide the same food as "classical" dormouse habitat in woodland, but is mostly strung out along hedgerows. Consequently, I have learnt relatively little about the ways of dormice here, compared with some of my other sites. However, work here has helped me realise the importance of competition for the boxes. Now that I am experimenting more at this site, competition is proving to be more and more a crucial factor.

I started a box scheme here in 1994 with fifteen boxes placed along the boundaries of an area of about 2ha of rough grazing, of which about a third is rather open scrub. In 1998 further boxes were added to comply with the requirements of the National Dormouse Monitoring Programme of having a minimum of fifty boxes. The number and positions of the boxes have varied over the years owing to ongoing hedgerow management. The habitats where boxes have been positioned have ranged from scrub with trees along an old track-way with no stock access, to more open scrub areas and old hedgerows with stock access, to recently laid hedges fenced off from the stock. Everywhere on the reserve, dormouse use of the boxes has been erratic and unpredictable. Few boxes are used, and few dormice are usually seen, at any one time, but 20-50 per cent of the boxes are used by dormice most years. The numbers of dormice seen at Kingcombe appear to place it among the better sites in the National Dormouse Monitoring Programme. It is, of course, impossible to make direct comparisons, as boxes in hedgerows cannot be placed in a grid as they can in woodland.

In the first year I was excited to see a dormouse twice during the year in the fifteen boxes. In the heat wave of the following year, 1995, by October there were sixteen dormice in the fifteen boxes! In 1995 and 1996 I compared this set of boxes with a further fifteen boxes in another area of the reserve with similar habitat. I was soon to start experiencing the "wood mouse effect." In 1995 I did not see any wood mice in the boxes until November, and then only in two boxes in each area. In 1996 I saw wood mice throughout the year; they used six of the boxes in the first area with twelve wood mice seen during the year. In the second area they used eight boxes, but a total of forty-two wood mice were seen. In the original site, with fewer wood mice, the dormice used ten boxes at some time during 1996, whereas at the site where I saw more wood mice they used only three boxes. The wood mice usurped several of the dormouse nests during the year and seemed to be the controlling force, whereas they seem to have ignored the boxes in the drier, hotter summer of 1995.

In subsequent years, when I had increased the number of boxes to over fifty, I did not see many more dormice than previously. I had inadvertently moved into habitats where dormice were far more reluctant to use boxes. More nest boxes were used by dormice in areas with

Kingcombe Meadows Reserve, showing the display of wild flowers in the unimproved grassland

A recently laid hedge at Kingcombe. Note the box hanging on the right hand fence post and a tube hanging from the wire near the left side of the photo. The dormice usually nested in the tubes rather than the boxes, as these were the preferred nesting places for wood mice

Living with Dormice

patches of hazel bushes, similar to the area where I had first started. Fewer nest boxes were used in such habitat as the well-wooded trackway. Initially it seemed that the use of boxes by dormice was poor where there appeared to be a better supply of natural nesting sites. However, I gradually realised that a more important controlling factor was the effect the various habitats had on the numbers of wood mice. Wood mice were found in the boxes more often where there was more undergrowth, but less often in habitats such as hazel bushes and old hedges, with little ground vegetation. So wood mice appeared to be the major controlling force, even though the use of boxes by wood mice at this site was much less than at any of my other sites, and was rarely above 20 per cent in any year.

It was unfortunate that I had no measurements of the populations of wood mice, which can fluctuate greatly, and could only judge them from the numbers found nesting in the boxes. Perhaps by merely visiting boxes wood mice may leave enough scent to stop dormice using them. Only rarely have I had a dormouse use a box that had been used by wood mice earlier in the year.

Kingcombe appears to be at the extreme westerly range of the yellow-necked mouse, a rather larger and more aggressive relation of the wood mouse. I did not see any sign of them until I found one in a box in 1999. The presence of yellow-necked mice, although I saw them in only relatively few boxes, seemed to be a major factor in lowering the number of boxes being used by dormice in both 2000 and 2001. I saw no signs of yellow-necked mice during 2002 and 2003, and the dormouse use of boxes improved. The following year saw the return of the yellow-necked mice, and the numbers of boxes used by dormice again fell. Yellow-necked mice appear to be even more arboreal in nature than wood mice. The boxes they targeted were mainly in the areas of the hazel bushes, which previously had been the boxes most frequented by dormice. I have found that the years when I saw fewest dormice (and hence lowest "dormouse populations" in official parlance) were when I saw most evidence of yellow-necked mice.

In 2004 I had started experimenting by leaving dormouse nests from the previous year in four of the boxes. In May I found only three boxes with new dormouse nests in, and two of these were in boxes containing old nest material; one of the other old nests had a wood mouse in it and the last one a yellow-necked mouse. This seemed to indicate that the presence of old nest material was a definite attractant to dormice, so long as some other competitor did not get there first.

After a trial run with five nest tubes in one of the hedges in 2004, when all the tubes ended up with dormouse nests in them, 2005 was a year for more experimentation. In two hedgerows I alternated ten boxes, hung on the fence posts, with ten tubes, hung on the barbed wire. When hanging boxes on fence posts I had previously learned the hard way not to hang boxes on posts where there were strainers, as these enable toads to climb up into the boxes, and then they are unable to get out again. The dormice started nesting in the boxes before there were any signs of them using the tubes. But in both hedgerows dormice nested in a single box only: wood mice later trashed both these nests. Wood mice and yellow-necked mice nested in several other boxes in the hedgerows. The results from the tubes were very different: by September dormice had used seven tubes in the first hedgerow and five in the second hedgerow. Unfortunately, the results were ruined by finding in October that someone had trashed fifteen of the tubes.

In areas of Kingcombe where there are hazel bushes with little undergrowth, dormice readily use the boxes but wood mice are rarely found

Trackway at Kingcombe. Here there is more undergrowth, and the boxes are mainly used by wood mice

Conclusions

The results nevertheless showed that there were numerous dormice around, but just too much competition and danger from other mice, for them to use the boxes.

The remaining forty-two boxes in 2005 were in more "wooded" areas, and included ten new boxes (would dormice like boxes never tainted by wood mice?). Four of the old boxes were seeded with dormouse nest from the previous year. Dormice nested in only ten of the forty-two boxes during the year, and these included all four of the seeded boxes but only one of the new boxes. Wood mouse use of the boxes was similar to that of most years, but that of yellow-necked mice was much higher and they were found in six boxes. This was the largest influx ever of yellow-necked mice into the boxes, and they were found in all types of habitat, including hedgerows. So perhaps it was not surprising that dormice used so few of the boxes. It was also notable that it was the first time in ten years that I did not find any families of young dormice in the boxes, and the October count was the worst ever, with only three dormice seen in sixty-two boxes. That the poor results in 2005 were due mainly to greater competition with other mice for the boxes, rather than a poor year for dormice, was shown by the greater activity of dormice in the tubes in the hedgerows.

By 2006 I had cut down to only fifty boxes. It did not seem possible that our studies at Kingcombe could show me more, but the hot dry summer of 2006 was to prove me wrong. School parties visiting the reserve found wood mice absent from their catches in traps for small mammals, and there were other reports that the numbers of wood mice were very low in the South West. By September I had not seen any other small mammals in the boxes, and in October saw only one pygmy shrew. This decrease in competition from other mice resulted in more dormice than usual being seen in the boxes. There were eight broods of young dormice, more than in any previous year, and so different from the year before, when I had not seen any. October produced almost twice as many dormice as I had ever seen before at any one time. Thirty-five dormice in the boxes and a further five in the tubes was a very pleasant change from the three of the previous year.

In 2006 I had been experimenting by seeding more of the boxes with nest material, and this had also helped boost the numbers of dormice using the boxes. At the beginning of the year, of the thirty boxes in the more "wooded" areas of the reserve, I seeded six boxes with dormouse nests, and six with hay. Both types of nest material had seemed attractive to dormice on other sites, and I wished to know which dormice preferred. By August dormice had nested in eight of the of twelve seeded boxes, but surprisingly both types of bedding seemed to be equally attractive to the dormice. In contrast they had nested in only four of the 18 "empty" boxes. The results confirmed that seeding boxes radically altered use of boxes by dormice. However, it does not seem that just having nesting material provided is the attractant, as the dormice almost invariably add their own fresh material, with which they make a new nest.

I then realised that it might not merely be what was attractive to dormice that was important, but the effect the bedding had on the other competitors for the nest boxes. It was fortuitous that other mouse numbers crashed in 2006, leaving tits as the only real competitors. As dormice often take over nests started by tits, I had not previously considered tits as competitors, but thinking again I had never known a dormouse take over a tit nest once the tit was at the stage of egg

above: Even in the hedgerows of Kingcombe dormice sometimes use stinging nettle leaves for nest building. These leaves just happened to be the ones nearest the box

top: Cattle grazing at Kingcombe

Living with Dormice

brooding, this could be a major factor that I had previously ignored. Tits had nested in only four of the seeded boxes, whereas they had at least started nests in sixteen of the eighteen "empty" boxes. It is significant also that the four "empty" boxes used by dormice initially included the two not nested in by tits. The other two boxes were not used until July, after the young tits had flown and their nests had been removed. The results seemed to indicate that seeding the boxes has a deterrent effect on nesting birds, and this could be a reason for the dormice choosing seeded boxes rather than "empty" ones.

It seemed surprising that stopping birds nesting in boxes was such an important factor. But it did not appear to be the only reason why seeding can attract dormice into boxes. I had found on other sites that seeding boxes in the autumn had the same effect. Seeding boxes later in the year may be important in deterring birds from using the boxes to roost in. By September only twelve of the thirty boxes remained free of dormouse nests. I left four of them empty, and seeded eight of them. Again it did not seem to matter which material was used for seeding. By November there were five new dormouse nests, four in boxes newly seeded in September and only one in an empty box. Obviously, numerous factors are involved in why seeding affects dormouse use of boxes and I have only been able to touch on them. However, the results of seeding help to show that, owing to various factors, the use of boxes by dormice from site to site, or even from year to year at the same site, is not comparable.

Without the normal pressure from wood mice, the results from the hedgerows in 2006 also proved interesting. There was less pressure from nesting birds in these boxes than in the more wooded areas, and tits only attempted to nest in eight of the twenty boxes. The dormice showed a distinct disinterest in the nest tubes compared with the previous years, but used more of the boxes. By September the dormice had nested in eight of the boxes in the hedgerows, including two with broods of young, but only in six of the tubes. From this it would appear that dormice may prefer boxes to nest in, but usually there is too much competition to make them safe nesting places.

Results from 2007 are as yet preliminary. I feared that the atrocious wet weather of the early summer might have been disastrous for dormice. However, by July there were good numbers in the boxes with weights as good as usual and some with flourishing broods of young. Dormice are indeed tough little beasts!

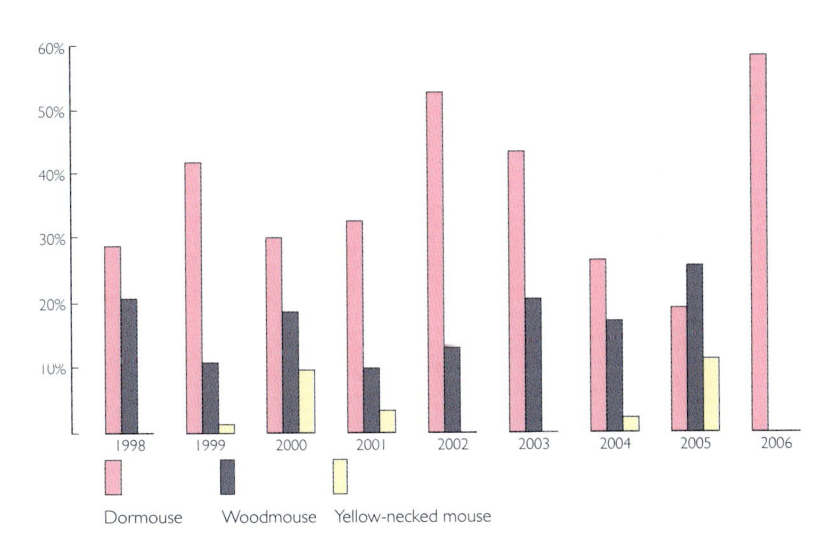

Comparison of numbers of nest boxes used by different species of mice on the Kingcombe Reserve between April and October each year. Many factors determine the use of boxes by dormice, but note how numbers tend to decrease in years when more boxes are used by wood mice, and the marked effect that the presence of yellow-necked mice seems to have

Our garden

The wild part of our garden lies behind the five beach huts on the left hand end of the row

It is in the coastal scrub behind the Chesil Bank that I discovered just how different the real dormouse is from the one in the literature. Earlier advice had been to look for dormice on the sheltered side of woods containing hazel. There is little, except sea, between the Chesil Bank and South America, and little other than blackthorn and bramble in the scrub. It was originally suggested to me that dormice were merely hanging on here as a relict population, but most of the scrub is of relatively recent origin, and I have found dormice to be widespread and plentiful in the area. Boxes were put up in our own garden and in a nearby reserve and dormice were found to be as abundant here as in any other habitat.

The wild part of our garden is roughly 0.3ha in size, and is one third of an area of blackthorn scrub that runs behind a row of beach huts. The scrub was originally composed almost entirely of impenetrable blackthorn with some bramble and wild privet. It was here in 1988 that Roy discovered two hibernating dormice, when using a brush cutter to clear land for a fence. By 1989 he had cut a series of pathways through the scrub and put up fifteen tit nest boxes. In 1994, when we had obtained licences to handle dormice, fifteen dormouse boxes were added. But still no signs of dormice in the boxes. Still we persevered and the tits were making good use of the boxes. The "eureka" moment did not come until 2nd December 1995, when I found a 30 gram male dormouse in one of the boxes – one of the old tit boxes of course!

An upturn in fortunes came in 1996, with a dormouse nest in a dormouse box in July, though no dormouse was found until October. A week later there were two new dormice in the box and another nest in an adjacent tit box. The next check in November produced a fourth dormouse in residence. Three days later, I realised that I had missed a box, and in it found the fourth dormouse again. I could hardly believe that it had put on 3 grams in three days. Further checks showed that at least seven different dormice had visited the original nest; the last one was not found until December. Only three of the thirty boxes had even had dormouse nests in them that year.

During the next few years a pattern emerged of an occasional dormouse using a box in the early spring, and then a few using the boxes in late autumn, often not until the winter storms had

Living with Dormice

torn most of the leaves from the bushes in late October or even November. The dormice seemed loath to use many of the boxes, and even more loath to breed in them. The first breeding nest that I found was in June of 1998, but contained seven dead, very young dormice, which were covered in small teeth marks. I suspected that this was the work of wood mice, as they were using many of the boxes.

Typically in 1999 only one dormouse was seen in the spring and nine in the autumn. Only six boxes were used all year, even though five more boxes had been put up beyond our garden, in a field along the back edge of the rest of the patch of scrub. In the autumn three of the dormice were found moving between boxes, but the prize went to one who was found twice to have alternated between the far end of the extension and the middle of our patch. That September I seeded four boxes with hay. Of the five boxes used that autumn, three were ones that I had seeded, another dormice had already nested in one that spring, and one was in the new extension.

By using more extensive seeding with hay in August 2000, I ended up with some 40 per cent of the boxes containing dormouse nests. The seeding did not actually help me see more dormice; seven dormice were seen that autumn, but nearly all were in nests first built in the spring. I had also been experimenting with using a few larger nest boxes and in June found a mother and four well grown young in one of them. Except for a mother with a single youngster, this was the only successful brood I have ever found in our garden in over ten years.

I suspected that it was competition with wood mice that was keeping dormice out of most of the boxes. Although all five boxes in the extension had dormouse nests in them in 2000, I gave them up in 2001, as all had been taken over subsequently by wood mice. This saved climbing over a thorn hedge using a rickety stepladder, and having to crawl under two lots of barbed wire fencing. Numbers of dormice seen in 2001 stayed much the same. One was seen in the spring, and seeding the boxes with hay produced two more nests by June. There was no more activity until October, when six more boxes were used and about nine more dormice seen. Numbers are vague here because for the first time there was a box that the dormice managed to shoot out of, before they could be trapped inside. The possible problem with this box was that it could only be reached from a slope above it, and therefore a quiet approach was more difficult. Boxes made of thicker wood may be advantageous to the surveyor (but not to the dormouse) as they may provide better soundproofing, which muffles approaching footsteps.

In 2002 I did not seed the boxes with hay. The year started well with four boxes with nests and four dormice seen. The boxes then seemed deserted until one dormouse was found in November. I had, however, been testing nesting tubes at the same time, so knew there were more dormice around that autumn. In sixteen tubes there were four dormouse nests and I had seen a good handful of dormice, but as with most tubes, the occupants had escaped so that I could not mark them and know true numbers. The dormice showed much greater willingness to use tubes during the summer months than they ever had the boxes.

In 2003 the boxes did badly despite seeding a few with actual dormouse nest; only two boxes, both seeded, were used during the year and five dormice seen. Nevertheless, the boxes proved interesting as they contained the only signs I had ever seen in the garden of yellow-necked mice. I only ever saw the suspect animal once and then only by torch light, when it disappeared into the bushes like a rocket, but the creature had filled a large nest box with over 4,000 dried blackberries and sloes. The animal came back and opened all the sloe stones by splitting them in two, not by making neat holes, as do wood mice and dormice.

Dormice have only ever bred in the bigger boxes in our garden. But not this one, because it is badly positioned, being easily accessed by wood mice

In 2004 four boxes were seeded with dormouse nest. In the autumn dormice were found in five boxes, two of which were the seeded nests used in the spring. From mid October to early December I caught and marked twenty-five different dormice in these boxes. Many were recaptured, but new ones appeared even up to the last sighting on 4th December. The highest number found at any one time was ten. Even with so many dormice being seen, wood mice still seemed to be the top dogs; of the five boxes in which wood mice were found that year, four had first been built in by dormice.

By 2005 I had halved the number of boxes. As dormice used so few of them, keeping fewer but in better condition and scrubbed out each year, seemed a better tactic. In the spring I seeded four boxes and was rewarded with new dormouse nests in all of them by May. The dormice used only one other box that spring, and I saw a total of five dormice. But wood mice were very abundant, not so much in the boxes during the summer as in the vegetable garden! There was no more dormouse activity in the boxes for the rest of the year, and even fresh seeding produced only wood mice. In desperation ten nest tubes were put up in October; by November I found one good dormouse nest with the remains of a dead rodent in it – even that proved to be a wood mouse! That this did not really signify a disastrous year for dormice, but rather a local problem with wood mice, seemed to be shown by other results I obtained locally. In the wooded garden of the Othona Community on the same coastal slope only 2km away I put up ten tubes in the middle of September, and a month later found six dormice in them.

In 2006 I found no dormice in the boxes in the spring, but then I had not carried out any winter cleaning or renovating of the boxes, so got the results I deserved! With a bit of cleaning and some seeding with hay the dormice were back in the boxes, but not until late October. But they were not back in the numbers that I had hoped. It seemed that the crash in wood mouse numbers was not as marked on the coast as inland, and the wood mice were back in force by October.

Only eleven boxes remained by 2007. With some cleaning and hay, these attracted six dormice by May. Hay does seem to attract the dormice, but whereas hay seems to deter most tits nesting in more wooded sites it does not in coastal scrub, as there are no alternative nest holes. Here in the larger boxes the tits will squash the hay down and build on top, but in smaller boxes the hay may even be removed and replaced by moss. I have just started experimenting with boxes with the entrance hole in the corner of the base of the box, rather than on a side. The only good new dormouse nest built in the spring of 2007 was built in such a box, even though it was not seeded with hay. This design should deter tits building nests, but whether it will deter wood mice, and their untidy nests, remains to be seen.

In most sites I have the problem of trying to tuck the boxes away so that they are not too obvious to the general public. On our own land I have had the advantage of not having to hide the boxes, and since found that the most obvious boxes were often the ones preferred by the dormice. One box that had never been used by dormice in years, was tucked in among the bushes. When Roy replaced it, he put the new box on a pole in front of the bushes. I thought it looked the silliest of places, but within two weeks there was a dormouse nest in it. Over the years dormice have proved me wrong so many times! It took thirteen years before I found a nest in another box that was only 6m away from the one used within two weeks. So often there seems to be no obvious reason why one box is used while another close by is ignored. Positioning of boxes can be critical: so I just keep looking and learning and being surprised by dormice.

The first tit box where dormice were found, six years after discovering that there were dormice in the area. It is still the favourite box of the dormice and used nearly every year

Living with Dormice

West Bexington Reserve

West Bexington is a nature reserve of the Dorset Wildlife Trust, only a short way on the other side of the village from our house. It consists of a large reed bed just behind the Chesil Bank, to the landward side of which is some meadowland and about 1.5ha of scrub. The scrub is mainly impenetrable blackthorn with some areas of willow. The boxes on this site often have to withstand full gale conditions. I started a nest box scheme here by putting up twenty boxes in February 1997. A month later wood mice were using five of the boxes, and by the end of the year fifteen boxes had been used and I had seen twenty-nine wood mice. But where were the dormice, which I knew were there from finding summer nests the previous autumn? It was not until the middle of November that I found two dormouse nests in the boxes. Checking again at the end of November I was lucky to come away with intact fingers, as in one of the nests was an angry weasel, with a larder of one wood mouse, two voles and just the tail end of a dormouse. So much for dormouse records; just one third of a young male, what a poor return for all the hard work, which included carrying all the boxes, eight foot poles and heavy tools along the beach to the site.

In 1998 results were better; dormice used seven of the boxes that year, and wood mice only four. Two dormice were seen in the spring, but then there were no signs of activity until late autumn when a further three dormice were seen. Worryingly though, in the spring a dormouse had been killed, presumably, from the teeth marks and state of the nest, by a wood mouse. In 1999 a similar pattern of records occurred, with five dormice seen in spring and five more in November. Again a wood mouse appeared to have attacked one of the dormice in the spring while it was in torpor, leaving two large areas of skin chewed away. Fortunately, we were in time to warm it up and Roy treated it with antibiotics. It soon made a good recovery.

In 2000 I tried seeding all the boxes with hay. By May there were six dormouse nests. But perhaps seeding was tempting dormice to use boxes against their better judgement! In one of the nests were six dead newly born dormice; in nine years of nest boxes on this reserve, this was the only time that dormice ever tried to breed in the boxes. Surprisingly, a phantom hay stealer removed all the hay in the boxes not used by tits or dormice. Could it have been dormice removing it for building wild nests? Only two dormice were seen that autumn, but a new, and rather unwelcome occupant of one box was a rat, which, after jumping in my face had the cheek to be in occupation again two months later. The rat had carried out adjustments to the entrance hole, but when I tried to fix a metal plate over it the following spring I was thwarted by finding a large family of pygmy shrews. Dormice boxes can certainly provide variety!

Visits to the boxes in 2001 did not start until June because of the foot-and-mouth restrictions. Only two dormouse nests were found, one with a dead wood mouse in it and the other taken over by bumblebees. No more dormouse signs were seen until a single nest was found in October. By 2002 some of the boxes were falling to pieces and five were replaced. By April dormice were found in three of the new boxes with all the old boxes ignored, but all these nests were usurped by wood mice during the summer. Typically for this coastal site, dormice did not use the boxes again until after a major storm at the end of October, when one box produced three juvenile dormice. But by 7th

Footpath between the reeds to the entrance of West Bexington Reserve. One year three dormice nests were found in the nearest patch of scrub — an area that floods every winter

West Bexington 2003. Problems with the neighbours as dormouse boxes made good rubbing posts and the stock pushed far into the scrub

November I was even more surprised to find seven youngsters of mixed ages, ranging in size from 7g to 27g, in the box. Several of these I met again during November, together with two others in another box. These dormice gave useful information on the weight gain before hibernation.

During 2002 I tested sixteen dormouse tubes in conjunction with the South West Dormouse Project. These I alternated with the boxes. The tubes, which had been placed on the outer branches of the bushes, seemed more acceptable to the dormice than did the boxes. By May four tubes had been built in and three dormice seen in them, but already a wood mouse had taken up residence in one of the nests. By the end of the year dormice had built in eleven of the sixteen tubes. Wood mice had trashed eight of the dormouse nests in the tubes at some stage during the year but showed no inclination to build their own nests in them. In the autumn I found that both dormice and wood mice had opened sloe stones in some of the empty tubes.

In 2003, having found that nest tubes seemed so attractive to dormice, I again put up sixteen of them, but cut down the number of boxes to ten. By the end of the year dormice had built in eleven tubes. Meanwhile the boxes had fared rather badly, but this was largely due to the summer drought and young cattle being put into the area. The cattle found the boxes excellent rubbing posts and knocked six of them to the ground.

In 2004 I cut down to only six boxes and ten tubes. In the spring dormice built in one box and four tubes, and six dormice were seen. Only two boxes were used in the autumn but sixteen different dormice were seen in them. The tubes again did well, with dormouse nests in seven of them. The dormice always seemed to prefer tubes for most of the season, but turned to boxes after the worst of the autumn storms. From the relatively few sightings of dormice during the year and the lack of breeding in the boxes, I can only assume that the dormice feel safer and prefer their own nest sites. This was brought home to me on 13th November, when I realised that there was a wild nest built only 75cm from a tube and 5m from a box, both of which had been built in by dormice that year. On closer examination two dormice shot out of the wild nest, but both the other nests were empty. On 27th November the wild nest was still intact, but all the nesting material had been removed from the tube and nest box.

I had hoped that tubes made safer nest sites for dormice than did boxes. In April 2005 I was horrified to find a dormouse had been dragged out of a tube and scalped by a set of tiny teeth. It was the third casualty that I had found on this site in spring and illustrates the danger of dormice being in a state of torpor at this time of year, as it leaves them sitting targets for wood mice. This vulnerability to attack had been the main reason for cutting down on the number of boxes on this site. In 2005 dormice used only one box in the spring and one in the autumn, with three dormice seen on both occasions. Dormice built in nine of the ten tubes and opened sloe stones in the only other one; wood mice trashed four of the nests during the year.

In 2006 I had only four boxes, but dormice used none of them in the spring, but this was hardly surprising as tits had nested in all of them. Dormice built in six of the tubes that year. In a tube in August I found the first live brood of young dormice that I had seen on this site in ten years of putting up boxes and five years of putting up nest tubes! This may have been a result of fewer wood mice being present that year. In the middle of November I saw five dormice still using the tubes, but no signs of dormice nests in any of the boxes. By the

View of West Bexington from the east. Dormouse nests have been found in the scrub on the right

In the isolated clump of scrub shown in the background, boxes attached to the willows only ever contained wood mice. But dormouse nests have been found in the surrounding brambles

beginning of December wood mice were back and had taken over several boxes and tubes, and even more surprisingly had built their own nest in an empty tube. This was the first time in five years that wood mice had nested in a tube on this site without a dormouse having built in it first. Not that it was much of a nest: with three wood mice, there was a lot more mouse than there was nest!

The coastal sites show an extreme example of dormice not wanting to use nest boxes in the summer. Even in the spring and autumn, when boxes must seem attractive in leafless shrubs at times of severe storms, it is only youngsters, who are presumably rather inexperienced, I find in the boxes. In most sites the take-up of boxes seems to decrease during the hottest months of the year. This is generally thought to be due to the microclimate in the boxes becoming more unpleasant during hot weather. But as it seems to be mainly youngsters that use the boxes, is it that by summer time most may be experienced enough to have found better and safer nesting sites, and those using boxes in the autumn are the inexperienced of the next generation? Only occasionally, and then only in late autumn after the winter storms have removed the leaves, is there ever a real insight into the abundance of dormice in the coastal sites.

View of the reserve from Chesil Beach

Conclusions 121

Ryewater Nursery

In most areas it is advisable to hide boxes from human eyes as far as is possible. I know of one surveyor who had some hundred boxes turned round by some kind-hearted soul, who no doubt thought that birds needed the hole on the outside. I have found in our garden that dormice seem to choose the more obvious boxes, placed where there is little contact with the shrubs. I was pleased when I was very kindly offered the opportunity to work on a private estate in the north of Dorset by Clive Farrell to whom I am most grateful for all his help and interest. His estate is so interesting to visit that, fortunately, I was not put off by the few, or even one year by the total lack of dormice in the nest boxes. Clive is vice president of Butterfly Conservation and breeds tropical butterflies. I had the wonderful experience of having electric-blue morpho butterflies settle on my hand in one of his greenhouses, whereas on visits to Central America I had only ever had fleeting glimpses of them in the jungle.

I started a small nest box scheme of thirty-four boxes here in 1999. To start with I placed most of the nest boxes in a small deciduous wood and along an old hedge. In the first year results were disappointing: by September there were just two dormouse nests, both in boxes in the wood. By October there were four juvenile dormice in one of these boxes and a wood mouse had taken over the other nest, but there was a new nest with one dormouse in the hedgerow. Little did I know when I started, how useful the negative results here would be in giving me greater understanding as to why on many sites dormice often ignore boxes. It seemed that on the wet clays of the Blackmore Vale, wood mice were even keener to use nest boxes than on other sites. By October, twenty-one of the boxes had wood mouse nests in and twenty-eight wood mice were found in occupation; a further three boxes in the wood were filled with acorns, which looked like the work of yellow-necked mice.

Nest box in the woodland at Ryewater Nursery. Wasps and bumble bees often take over boxes. Here hornets are complaining that the box is not large enough

By April 2000 there were already six boxes with wood mouse nests in, but this had only increased to seven by October. Dormice were again little in evidence and the only boxes they used were two in the wood. However, one male did condescend to use one box for five consecutive months and was replaced by four other dormice in October. I hoped for better results in 2001. In April I found three wood mouse nests, but disaster had struck and there were signs of weasel attacks, resulting in many dead tits. Such attacks continued for the next two months in boxes in all the areas, covering a long distance, right across one large field, the wood and then another field. Even the wood mice decided it was unsafe and no further mammal signs were seen in the boxes until late October, when only a single wood mouse and one pygmy shrew were found.

In 2002 dormice were back, but only in one of the woodland boxes, and plenty of wood mice were at home. It seemed time for some experimentation. I tried putting some boxes 4m up in some oak trees, but all to no avail as wood mice subsequently occupied them all. In August I removed some of the boxes being used by wood mice and placed four new clean boxes in the wood. Bingo! In October one of these boxes contained a nest with three dormice in it. But meanwhile in July I had put out some trial nest tubes, fifteen in the wood and five in the old hedge. There were never any signs of nests in the tubes in the wood, but in the hedgerow there was a nest with a dormouse by October and a second nest by November. So in the hedge in four months

Dormouse breeding nest in a tube in the hedge at Ryewater Nursery. It was difficult to get the nest back into the tube along with the mother and her six large young.

Living with Dormice

with five tubes, there was more evidence of dormice presence, than using twelve nest boxes for four years, when there had been only one nest box used by a dormouse in the first autumn. Subsequent years using tubes showed that there was a good population of dormice living in the hedge alongside the wood mice, and on one occasion a dormouse was found in a tube only 3m away from a box that contained a large family of wood mice.

In 2003 more experimentation was called for. In this and all subsequent years I used only boxes in the wood. In the wood I now had sixteen boxes, a mixture of old and clean new ones. Dormice nested in one of the new boxes in the spring, but later bred in an old box in which a nest had been left from the year before. In August I added four more boxes seeded with dormouse nest material. New dormouse nests were found in two of these in the autumn. In the hedge instead of boxes I had put sixteen nest tubes, and ten of these had dormice nests in them by October. On one occasion I even found a mother with six large young; trying to get them all back into the tube was almost an impossible task! She cannot have been too worried as she was found in a tube for a further two months, and she bred again. By December four of the dormouse nests in the tubes had been trashed by wood mice.

In 2004 only ten boxes were put in the woodland, five of these I seeded with dormouse nests. Dormice used two of these in the spring and another in the autumn together with one empty box. Wood mice were using four of the boxes by late autumn, including two that had been first built in by dormice. In 2004 I also returned ten clean boxes to the hedge and alternated them with ten tubes. In July there was one dormouse in a box, but his nest contained wood mice by the autumn. By November eight of the ten boxes in the hedge contained wood mouse nests. It seemed that by putting out clean boxes, dormice had been tempted to try and use them again in the hedge. Meanwhile, in the same part of the hedge, dormice had used half of the tubes by September. However, by October there was only one dormouse nest left (with dormouse) and six wood mouse nests (with three wood mice) in the tubes. Surprisingly, by early November dormice had built nests in two as yet unused tubes.

In 2005 I had only eight new boxes in the wood, which were arranged in pairs, and one of each pair was seeded with dormouse nest. One of the seeded boxes had a dormouse in it by May. Then there was the normal lull during July and August with no further activity, but by September three of the seeded boxes had new dormouse nests in them. The ten tubes in the hedge did well again that year with eight being used by dormice. By November the wood mice had as usual moved in and trashed seven of the dormouse nests in the tubes, but they had for the first time built one nest from scratch in a tube. One of the long term aims on this site was to see how soon dormice would move into newly planted scrub; nesting tubes seemed to be the answer. But in the area of new scrub I was thwarted, and for the second year running wood mice had built their own nests in all the tubes. This seemed to show the wood mouse's especial liking for areas with thick undergrowth, and hence tubes are unlikely to show the presence of dormice in such a habitat.

The presence of a dormouse nest in a box seemed to be a major attractant to other dormice. However, earlier tests at the coast had shown that even the presence of clean hay seemed to attract dormice. I decided to try to find out if dormouse nest, and presumably its associated scent, really attracted dormice more than just a clean box with hay. Duly in 2006 in the wood at Ryewater, I paired a box with hay with a box with dormouse nest collected the previous autumn. But wildlife has its own ideas: in the spring there were no dormice,

Hazel coppice woodland at Ryewater Nursery

above: More competition for the boxes in the woodland – here filled to the top with acorns by yellow-necked mice

below: Old hedgerow at Ryewater Nursery. Boxes in this hedgerow tend to be monopolised by wood mice, but tubes are readily used by dormice

and tits had chosen to nest in all the boxes seeded with dormouse nests and ignored the ones with hay. However, the negative results provided some interesting insights into the ways of tits, even if not into the ways of dormice. I looked back at the previous year's results and found the tits had then chosen the "empty" boxes and had ignored the boxes with dormouse nest material. All this surely illustrates the importance of not studying a species in isolation, and the importance of making full notes of all field observations, however unimportant they may seem at the time.

By October 2006 dormice had nested in five boxes and nine dormice were found. This was a record result for this wood. I suggest, though, that such good numbers of dormice were rather more due to the absence of wood mice in 2006, than to the experimental seeding of the boxes.

In contrast to the record results in the wood, the results in the tubes in the hedgerow were poorer than usual in 2006. Although dormice had nested in eight of the ten tubes during the year, in October only one dormouse was found to be in residence. This perhaps again showed that dormice are not that keen on tubes, unless they are being harassed by wood mice. With hindsight, I now know that it would have been more than interesting to have had boxes in the hedgerow in 2006, but I had unfortunately previously decided that wood mice had been provided with boxes for long enough in that hedge.

The explanation that I originally formulated as to why seeding attracts dormice in boxes was that dormice feel safer in boxes that smell of other dormice. This explanation is obviously too simplistic, and the effect that seeding has on competitors for boxes must also be taken into consideration. More experimentation is needed, but it would seem that nest boxes can endanger dormice rather than help them; and seeding boxes could further endanger their lives.

124 *Living with Dormice*

Abbotsbury Swannery

The nest box studies that I carried out at the Swannery at Abbotsbury are a salutary example of how long and how difficult it can be to prove that dormice are in any area using artificial nesting sites. The Swannery is home to one of the few colonies of mute swans in the world, scarcely, one would think, suitable habitat for dormice as well! Their presence here just shows how versatile, widespread and elusive they are. The Swannery is situated at the west end of The Fleet lagoon behind the Chesil Bank. Most of the land is reed-bed, but in places this is backed by willow carr and there are large trees on the drier areas. The whole area is subject to flooding during major storms; the last occasion was in 1989. The last report of dormice in the area was in 1983, before the last major flood. There are large grass fields inland of The Swannery with only one long narrow hedge forming any sort of arboreal linkage to further inland. I am grateful to the Ilchester Estates for giving me access to the area.

I set up thirty nest boxes early in 1998. And kept hoping. After five years I gave up hope with the boxes, which were getting older, and the stinging nettles seemed taller each year. However, having had such good results with nest tubes in coastal scrub, I roped in one of the staff to help with a set of sixteen tubes in 2003, in conjunction with the South West Dormouse Project. But it was not until October 2004 that I was asked to adjudicate on a nest in one of the tubes. Fortunately, it was easy: there was a dormouse in the tube, and two further dormice were seen in the same tube that autumn. The following year the results were again nil. In 2006 I tried again by putting clean tubes up in September. Again no sign of dormice, but hardly surprising as many of the tubes had been roosted in by birds, and in the tube near where I had seen dormice before was the nest of a yellow-necked mouse.

As I have gradually found out over the years, in such a wet habitat, tubes and boxes are a wonderful asset to wood mice, who are short of dry nesting places. This site had shown the problem of trying to survey an area with boxes or tubes placed at easily accessible heights, when most of the dense foliage is at the tops of the trees. It had taken seven years to prove that dormice were still there, but had they managed to survive the floods while in hibernation or are they good dispersers across farmland with very few hedges?

The winter of 2006-7 was, however, to prove that all the "monitoring" of dormice over the years was virtually in vain and useless compared with the ways of the old woodmen. A friend, Steve Hales, was coppicing a small area of willow carr behind the reed bed, to make clearance for mist nets, and in the process found six dormouse nests nestled in the stools of the willows. This was an area where boxes and tubes had over the years drawn a blank other than a toad, a family of pygmy shrews and many, many wood mice. The nests in the stools were up to a foot off the ground, which is a good thing, as exceptionally high Spring tides flood the area. This must surely be the first record of intertidal dormice! And that was not all, when checking for tits' nests in the handful of boxes which had been left over from dormouse monitoring – and were hence nine years old – Steve found a dormouse in a tit's nest. Not only was it the first record of a dormouse using a nest box at the Swannery, the box was merely attached to a chain-linked fence, against which no bushes make contact.

The Swannery. Dormice have been found both in the gardens and in the wet willow carr behind the reed beds. On the continent dormice have been reported nesting in reed beds

Dormouse nest in the stool of a coppiced willow, in an area that is flooded by the highest Spring tides

Conclusions   125

Bibliography

Anon, 1993. *The Great Nut Hunt*. Peterborough: English Nature.

Anon, 2001. *The Great Nut Hunt, 2001*. Peterborough: English Nature.

Battersby, J. (Ed.) & Tracking Mammals Partnership, 2005. *UK mammals: species status and population trends. First report by the Tracking Mammals Partnership.* Peterborough: JNCC/Tracking Mammals Partnership

Bright, P.W., 1996. *Status and woodland requirements of the dormouse in England*. English Nature Research Reports 166. Peterborough: English Nature.

Bright, P., 1997. "Helping the dormouse." *Enact* 5:12-15.

Bright, P., 1998. "Behaviour of specialist species in habitat corridors: arboreal dormice avoid corridor gaps." *Animal Behaviour* 56:1485-90.

Bright, P.W., 2000. *Status and Woodland Requirements of the Dormouse in Wales*. Countryside Council for Wales. Report 406, Bangor.

Bright, P. and MacPherson, D., 2002. *Hedgerow management, dormice and biodiversity*. English Nature Research Reports 454. Peterborough: English Nature.

Bright, P.W., Mitchell, P. and Morris, P.A., 1994. "Dormouse distribution: survey techniques, insular ecology and selection of sites for conservation." *Journal of Applied Ecology* 31:329-39.

Bright, P.W. and Morris, P.A., 1990. "Habitat Requirements of Dormice *Muscardinus avellanarius* in Relation to Woodland Management in Southwest England." *Biological Conservation* 54:307-326.

Bright, P.W. and Morris, P.A., 1991. "Ranging and nesting behaviour of the dormouse, *Muscardinus avellanarius*, in diverse low-growing woodland." *Journal of Zoology (London)* 224:177-90.

Bright, P. and Morris, P., 1993a. "Conservation of the Dormouse." *British Wildlife* 4:154-62.

Bright, P.W. and Morris, P.A., 1993b. "Foraging behaviour of dormice *Muscardinus avellanarius* in two contrasting habitats." *J.Zool.,Lond.* 230:69-85.

Bright, P.W. and Morris, P.A., 1995. "A review of the dormouse (*Muscardinus avellanarius*) in England and a conservation programme to safeguard its future." *Hystrix(n.s.)* 6:295-302.

Bright, P.W. and Morris, P.A., 1996. "Why are dormice rare? A case study in conservation biology." *Mammal Review*. 26:157-187.

Bright, P. and Morris, P. 2002. "Putting Dormice back on the map." *British Wildlife* 14: 91-100.

Bright, P.W. & Morris, P.A. 2005. *The Dormouse.* London: The Mammal Society.

Bright, P.W., Morris, P.A. and Mitchell-Jones, A.J. 1996a. "A new survey of the Dormouse *Muscardinus avellanarius* in Britain, 1993-4." *Mammal Review* 26:189-95.

Bright, P., Morris, P. & Mitchell-Jones, A. 1996b. *The dormouse conservation handbook*. Peterborough: English Nature.

Bright, P., Morris, P. & Mitchell-Jones, A. 2006. *The dormouse conservation handbook*. Second edition. Peterborough: English Nature.

Buchner, S., 1997. "Common dormice in small isolated woods." *Natura Croatica* 6:271-74.

Chanin, P. & Woods, M., 2003. *Surveying dormice using nest tubes. Results and experiences from the South West Dormouse Project*. English Nature Research Report No.524. Peterborough: English Nature.

Delany, M.J. (ed.), 1985. *Yorkshire Mammals*. Bradford, University of Bradford.

Eden, S. & Eden, R., 1999. "Dormice in Dorset – the importance of hedges and scrub." *British Wildlife.* 10:185-189.

Eden, S.M. & Eden, R.M.G., 2001. "The dormouse in Dorset; a reappraisal of dormouse ecology." *Proceedings of the Dorset Natural History and Archaeological Society.* 123, 75-94.

Eden, S.M. & Eden, R.M.G. 2003. "Further observations on dormice in Dorset." *Proceedings of the Dorset Natural History and Archaeological Society* 125:125-129.

Garland, L. and Woods, M., 2005. "Dormice on Road Verges." *In Practice (Bulletin of the Institute of Ecology and Environmental Management).* 48:2-6

Hambler, C. and Speight, M.R., 1995. "Biodiversity conservation in Britain: Science replacing tradition." *British Wildlife.* 6:137-47.

Hurrell, E., 1962. *Dormice*. Animals of Britain 10: Sunday Times Publications.

Hurrell, E., 1980. *The Common Dormouse*. Blandford Press.

Hurrell, E. & McIntosh, G., 1984. "Mammal Society dormouse survey, January 1975-April 1979." *Mammal Review*. 14:1-18.

Irving, A., 2001. "New Dormouse records for Kingbury Wood." *Sanctuary* 30:77.

Jermyn, D.L., Messenger, J.E. & Birks, J.D.S., 2001. *The distribution of the hazel dormouse* Muscardinus avellanarius *in Wales*. Ledbury: The Vincent Wildlife Trust.

Joss, W., 2001. "Jack and the dormouse." *Natur Cymru* 1:14-17.

Juškaitis, R., 1995. "Relations between Common Dormice (*Muscardinus avellanarius*) and other occupants of bird nest-boxes in Lithuania." *Folia Zoologica* 44(4):289-296.

Juškaitis, R., 1997a. "Use of nestboxes by the common dormouse (*Muscardinus avellanarius* L.) in Lithuania." *Natura Croatica* 6:177-188

Juškaitis, R., 1997b. "Breeding of the common dormouse (*Muscardinus avellanarius* L.) in Lithuania." *Natura Croatica* 6:189-197.

Juškaitis, R., 1999. "Winter mortality of the Common Dormouse (*Muscardinus avellanarius*) in Lithuania." *Folia Zoologica* 48(1):11-16.

Morris, P., 2004. *Dormice*. Stowmarket: Whittet Books.

Morris, P.A., Bright, P.W. and Woods, D., 1990. "Use of nest boxes by the Dormouse *Muscardinus avellanarius*." *Biological Conservation* 51:1-13.

Oxford, G., 2007. "The hazel dormouse (*Muscardinus avellanarius*): re-introduction to North Yorkshire." *Naturalist* 132:3-8.

Pitt, F., 1937. "The Acrobat of the Bushes," in F. Pitt, ed., *The Romance of Nature* 1:111-120. London: Country Life.

Rackham, O. 1986. *The History of the Countryside*. London: Dent.

Richards, C.G.J., White, A.C., Hurrell, E. and Price, F.E.F. 1984. "The food of the common dormouse, *Muscardinus avellanarius*, in South Devon." *Mammal Review* 14:19-28.

Summers, A., 2001. "Botany, Salisbury Plain training area (East) Bulford Wiltshire." *Sanctuary* 30:81.

Tattersall, F. and Whitbread, S., 1994. "A trap-based comparison of the use of arboreal vegetation by populations of bank vole (*Clethrionomys glareolus*), woodmouse (*Apodemus sylvaticus*) and common dormouse (*Muscardinus avellanarius*)." Communications from the Mammal Society No.68. *Journal of Zoology*, London 233:314-317.

Tickell, O., 1995. "Exotic tastes. Dormouse future depends on the sycamore tree." *BBC Wildlife* 13(10):23.

Vaughan, G., 2001. "'Dormousitis' – the sequel or should tit boxes be erected for birds or mammals?" *Devon Birds* 54:3-17.

Vaughan, G., 2002. "'Dormousitis'– delight or dilemma?" *BTO News* 240:23-24.

Vogel, P., 1997. "Hibernation of recently captured *Muscardinus, Eliomys* and *Myoxus*: a comparative study." *Natura Croatica* 6:217-31.

Wheeler, B.R., 2000. *Conserving dormouse* Muscardinus avellanarius *population in the Weald*. English Nature Research Reports 362. Peterborough: English Nature.

Whitbread, 1986. "The Aerial Dormouse." *BBC Wildlife*, December 1986:599-602.

Wood, J.G., 1862. *The Illustrated Natural History. Mammalia*. London: Routledge Warne and Routledge.

Woodroffe, G.L., 2006. "Wildlife Reports: Mammals." *British Wildlife* 17:270-272.

Woods, D.E., 1997. "Nest boxes, captive breeding and re-introduction of the common dormouse (*Muscardinus avellanarius*) in England." *Natura Croatica* 6:199-204.

Yalden, D., 1999. The History of British Mammals. London: Poyser

The Dormouse Monitor is the Newsletter of the National Dormouse Monitoring Programme. Originally produced by P. Bright and P. Morris at Royal Holloway University of London it is now produced by The People's Trust for Endangered Species, 15 Cloisters House, 8 Battersea Park Road, London SW8 4BG. www.ptes.org

PTES News is the Newsletter of The People's Trust for Endangered Species.

Mammal News is the Newsletter of The Mammal Society, 2B Inworth Street, London SW11 3EP. www.mammal.org.uk

Juškaitis, R. 2008. *The Common Dormouse Muscardinus avellanarius: Ecology, Population Structure and Dynamics*. Institute of Ecology of Vilnius University Publishers, Vilnius. This recent publication gives good coverage of dormouse research on the Continent, a feature that is generally lacking in British literature.

Footnotes

THE COMMON DORMOUSE

The elusive dormouse
[1] *The Dormouse Monitor*, Winter 2004

Distribution of dormice in Britain
[1] Wood 1862
[2] Yalden 1999
[3] Hurrell and McIntosh 1984
[4] *The Dormouse Monitor*, October 2000
[5] Irving, 2001
[6] C. Turtle, pers. comm.
[7] *The Dormouse Monitor*, April 2003
[8] Vaughan 2001 and 2002
[9] J. Crowden, pers. comm.
[10] *The Dormouse Monitor*, April 2001

What does the dormouse eat?
[1] Richards et al. 1981
[2] Whitbread 1986
[3] Ozanne in Ticknell 1995
[4] Pitt 1937
[5] Joss 2001
[6] Vaughan 2001
[7] Juškaitis 1995
[8] Eden and Eden 2001

Habitats used by dormice
[1] Pitt 1937
[2] Eden and Eden 2001
[3] Chanin and Woods 2003

Deciduous Woodland
[1] Vaughan 2001 and 2002

Scrub
[1] *The Dormouse Monitor*, April 2003
[2] J. Crowden, pers. comm.

Hedges
[1] Chanin and Woods 2003
[2] Rackham 1986

Dormice in buildings
[1] Hurrell 1962
[2] *The Dormouse Monitor*, April 2002

Dormouse tolerance of human disturbance
[1] D. Woods, pers. comm.

Movement and dispersal of dormice
[1] Eden and Eden 1999 and 2001
[2] L. Sadlier, in Garland and Woods 2005
[3] Buchner 1997

Dormouse Nests
[1] *The Dormouse Monitor*, April 2002
[2] Wood, 1862
[3] *The Dormouse Monitor*, Spring 2006
[4] D. Woods, pers. comm.

Hibernation
[1] Hurrell 1962
[2] Wood 1862
[3] Woods 1997
[4] Eden and Eden 2003
[5] Vogel 1997

Summer torpor
[1] Pitt 1937

Breeding in dormice
[1] Vaughan 2001 and 2002
[2] Juškaitis 1997b

Predation of dormice
[1] Juškaitis 1999

It's a mouse eat mouse world
[1] D. Woods pers. comm.
[2] Tattersall and Whitbread 1994

SURVEYING FOR DORMICE
[1] Jermyn et al. 2001

Searching for hazel nuts eaten by dormice
[1] Eden and Eden 2001

Searching for dormouse nests
[1] Hurrell & McIntosh 1984

Providing artificial nesting sites for dormice
[1] Morris et al. 1990

Nest boxes for dormice
[1] Juškaitis 1997a
[2] Juškaitis 1995
[3] *The Dormouse Monitor* 1998
[4] Vaughan 2001 and 2002

Nesting tubes for dormice
[1] Chanin and Woods 2003

OTHER STUDIES ON DORMICE IN BRITAIN
[1] Hurrell 1962 and 1980
[2] Hurrell and McIntosh 1984
[3] Richards et al. 1984

A Mad Hatter's tea party?
[1] Bright et al. 2006
[2] Bright and Morris 2005
[3] Bright 1997

The Nut Hunts: finding the distribution of dormice in Britain
[1] Bright et al. 1994
[2] Bright 1996
[3] Bright et al. 1996a
[4] Hurrell and McIntosh 1984
[5] Bright and Morris 1996
[6] *Endangered British Mammals* (a PTES publication), No. 5, Autumn-Winter 1998
[7] *PTES News*, Summer 2003
[8] Anon 1993
[9] Anon 2001
[10] Jermyn et al. 2001
[11] Bright et al. 2006

Nest boxes and the National Dormice Monitoring Programme
[1] Bright and Morris 1996
[2] Bright and Morris 1993a
[3] Battersby 2005
[4] Bright et al. 1996b
[5] Woodroffe 2006
[6] Morris et al. 1990

Nesting tubes
[1] Bright and MacPherson 2002
[2] *PTES News*, Summer 2003

The numbers game
[1] Bright and Morris 2005
[2] Bright, in Battersby 2005
[3] *The Dormouse Monitor*, April 2002
[4] *The Dormouse Monitor*, 1998
[5] *The Dormouse Monitor*, Summer 2007
[6] *Mammal News*, Spring 2006

Breeding potential of dormice
[1] Bright and Morris 1996
[2] Bright and Morris 2005
[3] Bright and Morris 1993a
[4] Juškaitis 1997b

Food
[1] Bright and Morris, 1993b
[2] Bright and Morris, 1996
[3] Bright and Morris, 2005
[4] Bright and Morris, 1993a
[5] Bright, 1997
[6] Ozanne in Tickell, 1995
[7] Eden and Eden, 2003

Habitat
[1] Bright 1997
[2] Morris 2004
[3] Bright and Morris 1996
[4] Bright and Morris 2005
[5] *The Dormouse Monitor*, Spring 2005

Dormouse presence in conifer plantations
[1] Bright and Morris 2005

Dormouse presence in hedges
[1] Morris 2004
[2] Bright and MacPherson 2002
[3] Bright in publicity from PTES, March 2000

Dispersal of dormice; sink or source populations
[1] Bright 1997
[2] Bright and Morris 1991
[3] Bright and Morris 1996
[4] Bright et al. 2006
[5] *The Dormouse Monitor*, Winter 2005
[6] Bright 1998
[7] Wheeler 2000
[8] Bright et al. 1994
[9] Bright 1996

Problems with the British climate
[1] Bright and Morris 1996
[2] Morris 2004,
[3] Bright in Battersby 2005

Conservation action for dormice
[1] Bright and Morris 1993a
[2] Bright and Morris 1996
[3] Bright and Morris 2002

Management of habitat: to coppice or not to coppice
[1] Hurrell and McIntosh 1984
[2] Bright and Morris 1996
[3] Bright 2000
[4] Bright and Morris 1995
[5] Hambler and Speight 1995
[6] Bright et al. 2006
[7] Summers 2001

Managing conifers
[1] R. Trout in Bright et al. 2006

Reintroductions
[1] Bright and Morris 2002
[2] Irving 2001
[3] Oxford 2007
[4] Delany 1985
[5] *The Dormouse Monitor*, Autumn 2006

Postscript

My 2008 observations were made after I had submitted the manuscript of this book: they produced some salutary results. After many years of studying dormice, I had stupidly thought that I could predict the use of dormice boxes and knew where to look for wild nests. The dormice were having none of this.

Hunting for wild nests at the end of 2008, I only managed to find a couple of nests in an area where I had previously found 80 or more without undue effort. In contrast, there had been two broods of large young in boxes in our garden, when only one other had been seen in the pervious 18 years. It seems likely that both these results could have been due to the atrocious weather of the summer, especially the gales. Relatively exposed sites would have been useless for wild nests, and in desperation the dormice risked dry boxes for breeding, while normally they avoid them because of the wood mouse activity.

Such results emphasise that an area needs studying for several years before any conclusions are drawn about the presence of dormice, let alone any guess made at the numbers there.

Over a dozen dormice nests were found along the edge of this scrub in late 2007. In late 2008 not a single one was to be seen

Acknowledgments

I would like to thank all the landowners, especially the Dorset Wildlife Trust, Clive Farrell and the Ilchester Estates for giving me permission to work on their land. I am indebted to many people for showing me their monitoring sites and for discussing their work with me, particularly I would like to mention members of the Dorset Dormouse Group, staff of Forest Enterprise, Jan Crowden, Dr Cathy Turtle, and the late Doug Woods and Gordon Vaughan. I gratefully acknowledge the permission to include images taken by Steve Hales, Mike Read and Simon Knight. I thank Dr Phil Stirling and Nick and Caroline Tomlinson for their helpful comments on an earlier draft of this book. I am grateful to my publisher, Andreas Papadakis and his staff for their diligence in helping to produce this book, especially Sheila de Vallée for editing and Alexandra Papadakis for design. It was with great sadness that Andreas died in June 2008. Alexandra took over the completion of the publication of this book.

Photo Credits

All photos by Sue Eden except for the following:
Pages 2, 26, 33 (bottom right), 34, 43, 59, 62-3, 103 (top right) © Mike Bailey and Steve Williams. Pages 10, 61(top right), 64, 99, 100, 110 © Mike Read (www.mikeread.co.uk). Page 18 (bottom left) © Andrew Mawby. Page 29 (top right) © Tristan Bantock. Page 29 (bottom right) © Rachel Scopes. Pages 75, 125 (bottom right) © Steve Hales. Pages 13, 116 © Simon Knight.

128 *Living with Dormice*